Please return / renew by date shown.
You can renew at: **norlink.norfolk.gov.uk**
or by telephone: **0344 800 8006**
Please have your library card & PIN ready.

9/10/15 Dead Stock

**NORFOLK LIBRARY
AND INFORMATION SERVICE**

Secrets of an Essex Girl

Secrets of an Essex Girl

Lauren Goodger

HODDER &
STOUGHTON

GOO

First published in Great Britain in 2013 by Hodder & Stoughton
An Hachette UK company

1

A CIP catalogue record for this title is available from the British Library

Hardback ISBN 978 1 444 77017 9
Trade paperback ISBN 978 1 444 77019 3
eBook ISBN 978 1 444 77018 6

Typeset by Palimpsest Book Production Ltd, Falkirk, Stirlingshire
Printed and bound by CPI Group (UK) Ltd, Croydon CR0 4YY

Hodder & Stoughton policy is to use papers that are natural, renewable and
recyclable products and made from wood grown in sustainable forests. The
logging and manufacturing processes are expected to conform to the
environmental regulations of the country of origin.

Hodder & Stoughton
A division of Hodder Headline PLC
338 Euston Road
London NW1 3BH

www.hodder.co.uk

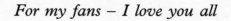

For my fans – I love you all

Contents

Acknowledgements

THANK YOU TO all my friends. You are like family to me. You know who you are and you mean everything. Trust is so important in this game and I trust you guys with my life. In particular, Lisa – you have been like a mum and a friend all rolled into one and I can't thank you enough for being there for me. There have been plenty of dark days, but you know what? With your help I'm turning the corner. Big love.

A great big thank-you to my fans – your belief in me makes me stronger every day.

To my management, Max Clifford Associates, for taking me on. I know you weren't sure at the beginning, but I changed your opinion of me, didn't I? You're not just my agents; you are my friends. Chloe, you're wicked.

Thanks to Hannah Fernando. You are amazing and

so patient, and we've had a giggle. I can't thank you enough for helping me write this book. Some of the subjects haven't been easy. I really appreciate all your hard work.

To the media: you're a bunch of bastards, but our love–hate relationship keeps things entertaining.

And finally to Fenella Bates and all at Hodder & Stoughton, for having faith in me.

Foreword

OH. MY. GOD. I can't believe I am writing my own book! It's totally mad what's happened over the last few years. I've gone from being a normal girl from Essex to suddenly being the focus of attention. It's both weird and amazing. My life has taken me down a completely different path and my feet have barely stopped to touch the ground. It's manic. Oh. My. God. It's manic!

Although my day-to-day life has changed, I don't think I've changed much as a person. For sure I've learned to have thicker skin and to try not to take things to heart as much, and I'm probably not quite so trusting with the banter I have with people in case they sell a story, but underneath it all, I would say I am the same girl I always was – bubbly and happy. Some of my insecurities have grown, and some I am finally learning to deal with, but I know I'm very lucky. Every day that goes by, I wake up feeling as though I am starting a new chapter in my life, as a single girl looking to the future. I have everything to look forward to. ☺

I'm quite different to the girl you think you know. People have watched *The Only Way Is Essex* and have understandably formed their own views about me. I was a character who divided opinions and I believe I was portrayed in a particular way. I don't think that the character that's been painted on *The Only Way Is Essex* is very fair, though, and I hope that when you've finished reading this book you'll think differently of me.

I want you to get to know me. The real me. The Lauren Rose Goodger behind closed doors and away from the cameras, not the one being judged on weight gain and weight loss, or the girl who is with Mark Wright and then isn't any more. There's a lot more to me than that. I am a human being just like you. I hurt the same, cry about the same things and laugh the same – it's just that nowadays I do it all in public. Some days it feels as though I can't cough without it being reported! I wouldn't be normal if things didn't get to me sometimes, and when I'm scrutinised for what I eat, what I don't eat and all that rubbish, it can occasionally drag me down. There are moments when I'd quite like to shut the door on it all – such as when Mark cheated on me and when we split up and every detail was shared with the world. I have some dark days when I question everything, but the good days without question far outweigh the bad. Please don't think I'm complaining – I'm not. I am very lucky and privileged to lead the life I do, and at this moment in time I am finding confidence I never knew existed in me. I am learning to like myself and to try and give myself a break. It's the beginning of a new phase in my life that I can finally be in control of. On the whole, I honestly don't have much to moan about. I'm living the life I always dreamed of and I'm having the best time. I'm loving it. 👍

I do sometimes worry that some people don't particularly like me. They have watched a person who in a way even I don't recognise and that bothers me. Perhaps that's down to my own insecurities – I need to feel liked and loved – but it is genuinely how I feel. Hopefully people's opinion of me is about to change. *fingers and toes crossed* Now, in this book, I finally have the opportunity to set the record straight in my own words and to tell my story from the beginning. My unconventional childhood, turning to Mark when I was just fifteen years old, cat fights, fallings out with producers on *TOWIE*, weight battles, my unhealthy attitude towards food and my daily struggle with my body image . . . it's time to lift the lid on it all. Scream! Hold tight – it's a rollercoaster ride!

1

It Wasn't Easy Growing Up as
Lauren Goodger

MY UPBRINGING WASN'T very conventional, to say the least, and I find it quite hard to open up about it. In fact, this is the first time I have. When I was a year old, my mum and dad broke up and Dad moved out of our family home in Bethnal Green, London. People ask me why, but the truth is, I don't know and have never asked. I don't need to know or want to know – I was too young to remember the split or even them being together in the first place, and it's not something I feel I need to know details about. It happened and Mum and Dad split up. That's the end of it as far as I am concerned.

Although I don't remember the split because I was so young, the aftermath of their separation has had a massive impact on me as a person. I guess it had to.

Until I was four, I lived with my mum in Bethnal Green but then Mum decided that it was best for me if I went to live with my dad in Redbridge, Essex, where he now had a house with his new girlfriend, Julie. Mum felt he could provide for me better than she could, and as hard as she says it was for her and for me, that's what happened. Mum tells me now how she felt really guilty about giving me to him and still does, and that she thinks I resent her for doing it, but at the time she truly thought it was for the best and that I would have a better start in life.

Now, this is where it gets confusing because my mum already had two kids by someone else, Nicola [she is three years older than me] and Anthony – or Tony, as we call him – who is four years older than me, so moving in with Dad meant not only leaving my mum but leaving my half-brother and -sister too. Mum had been with their dad from a really young age, but not long after Tony had been born, he'd upped and left. I don't even know his name and again I have never asked any questions. You are probably wondering why I don't ask or want to know about these things, but it doesn't matter. He's not around and that's the bottom line. I don't feel like I need to know any more. Besides, they don't have anything to do with him now and they have always lived with my mum.

As I was only four when I moved in with Dad, I don't remember being dropped off or the first night I slept in my new bedroom, and Mum has never spoken to me about it apart from saying how guilty she felt. I'm not sure whether me not remembering stuff is a kind of defence mechanism. It's like my mind has made sure that that period of my life is blocked out because it was such a horrible and difficult time for me. Although I can't remember any details, I know now that it must have been traumatic. It would be for any four-year-old who's been used to having their mum put them to bed every night. Just think about it – one day I was living with my mum, in her house in Bethnal Green, with her rules, her routine, and the next I was somewhere else, with a dad I had barely lived with before and his new girlfriend. I don't want to sound pathetic, but it makes me sad when I think about it and what I must have gone through.

Once I moved in with Dad, I only saw Mum on weekends, which was hard for both of us. Though it was only about half an hour from where my mum had moved to in Chigwell to my dad's in Redbridge, even getting to see me at weekends was a battle, she said. Apparently I was always busy doing some activity or other and it was really hard for her to get time with me. She doesn't drive, so she would make the trip on the number 167 bus each Saturday, collect me and I'd stay with her until Sunday night. After tea, we would get back on the bus and I'd go back to Dad's for the week. I remember never wanting to go back. I'd cry and cry because I wanted to stay with my mum. I missed her and longed to be with her. Going to bed at night in a different house and adjusting to my dad and Julie's routines was unsettling. For a time I recall crying every night for my mum, particularly after a weekend with her when I went back to Dad's. When I visited at weekends and saw Mum, Nicola and Tony all together like one big, happy family, I wanted to be part of it. I think any child would find it hard being separated from their mum and siblings, and I was no different.

It was upsetting and confusing for me going from one house to another and not being allowed to stay where I really wanted, but at the time it was just the way it was and I knew nothing else. I was too young to understand why I wasn't with Mum any more, but like all children do, I got on with it. There was no other option.

Mum, like Dad, had a three-bedroom semi, but they were so different. Hers was very warm and cosy and welcoming. Mum was, and still is, incredibly house-proud, but even though it was tidy, it always had a nice homely feel about it. I can remember she had really lovely carpets and sofas, and I felt at home there. Dad's was similar in size, but it was pretty basic. It didn't have welcoming soft furnishings like Mum's; it was more practical. It was just a normal house really. I was lucky, though, because he had a big garden, which I loved spending time in.

My dad, bless him, did everything he could to help me settle in and to give me a good life. He spent ages decorating my room in pink and cream, and he had a cabin bed made for me with my name engraved on it, which I loved. In the garden he put in a pond with a bridge over it so I could play, and he even built me my very own playhouse with a real front door! The front door was my nanny Jan's (my dad's mum) old front door, so you can imagine how big and realistic it was. I loved it and used to play in there for hours. It was every girl's dream. If we had a free weekend, Dad would build something for me to play with in the garden; he was really clever.

To be fair, Dad always made me his priority. When I went to live with him, he became my everything. In a way I suppose he became a mum and a dad for me during the week, but he wasn't really very cuddly, while Mum was always affectionate and touchy-feely. He'd give me a cuddle now and again, but he isn't someone who finds it easy to show love. Neither was Julie, which was hard for me, because if I'm feeling down or upset, that's all I want. I love cuddles and kisses, and when I'm a mum, my children will never go without that affection. ☺

Julie's mum, my nan Phyllis, was more affectionate. She is a lovely lady and I spent a lot of time with her over the years. She always tells me about when she first met me. She says I went running up to her front door, which was glass, put my mouth up against it and did this kind of raspberry thing that left a mark! She says I was a bubbly and loving child, and she returned that in spades.

Dad had met Julie not long after he split with Mum. Julie is completely different to my mum – in every way they are like opposites – and because she didn't have children of her own, she put all her efforts into me. Although I didn't particularly appreciate it at the time, Julie really did try and give me the best start in life. It was just different to what I had been used to with my mum. I can't remember the first time I met Julie – I was too young – but even at four years old, I think I knew that she couldn't replace my mum, and perhaps that's why we never really became that close. On those down days that everyone has, when only your mum will do, I was no different except I had to wait until the weekend to see my mum. Julie might have been doing everything for me and caring for me as a mum would, but the bottom line was that she wasn't my mum.

Right from the beginning the differences between life at Mum's and life at Dad's were very apparent. During dinnertimes at Dad's I'd be made to sit round the table with them and there was no way I was allowed to watch TV. I think I was only ever allowed to watch the kids' channels as a real treat or on special occasions. At Mum's I was allowed a telly in my bedroom, but there was no way Dad or Julie was gonna allow that. No way! Instead I had a keyboard piano and a karaoke machine to amuse myself with.

Julie wanted me to read and write and do proper educational things, even in my spare time, whereas my mum was happy for me to be a kid and play. Julie was the one who taught me to read and write. She might not have been physically very affectionate with me, but she wanted me to fulfil my potential.

At Dad's I would also have to earn my pocket money by doing chores around the house like washing up and helping with the housework. When I was at my mum's, though, she did everything. She wouldn't care if I got up in the morning and ate a bag of sweets for breakfast. If we went out, I'd be allowed fizzy drinks and crisps – whatever I wanted – rather than eating healthily like

I had to at Dad's. She didn't care what the hell I did. She thought the whole being strict thing was a load of rubbish and that kids should be kids. She used to clean for us and wash our clothes, while we didn't have to lift a finger.

I recall some stupid things that make me laugh now – for instance, I was never allowed bubble gum or chewing gum because Julie and Dad said it was common, so I'd have to have it over at Mum's, and if I brought any back, I'd have to stash it away so they didn't find it. I used to stay with my mum's mum, Nanny Pat, quite a bit when I was younger and she used to buy me bubble gum and those dummy sweets, which I wasn't allowed either. I was allowed all those things when Mum or Nanny Pat was about, but at my dad's it was against the rules. It's funny because when my mum came to round my flat not so long ago, she went into one of my kitchen cupboards and saw a stash of Hubba Bubba and it made her laugh. She was like, 'You've still got a fixation with the stuff and you're an adult now!' It's true – I bloody love it! ☺

Once I was at school, Dad and Julie were particularly strict when it came to doing my homework. Ah, I hated it! Julie had a good job herself in the city and would sit with me every evening so I got it all done and then she would read with me. It always felt like I had to be doing something that furthered me or was educational. Julie would encourage me to have lots of interests. She had me part of every club going! My time was filled with gymnastics, netball, reading, and going to Theatre Train on Saturday mornings, a theatre school in Chelmsford, where I learned to dance, act and sing. I really enjoyed acting, and Julie's mum, Nan Phyllis, used to pay for me to go. I can remember being a member of the cast in *Grease* at the Kenneth More Theatre. Although I was just part of a group and didn't have a specific character, I pretended every night that I was Sandy. Each performance I would imagine myself as the leading lady. I was in my own fantasy world and was at my happiest when I was on stage performing. I think it was an escape for me and I could get away from everything and all my worries.

Dad is a tiler by trade and has his own business, which going by the life we had, he always did well from. Materially I had pretty much everything I ever wanted living at my dad's. I didn't go without at all, but I still couldn't ignore the pull I felt to be with my mum. It wasn't that I hated living with my dad, although I didn't love it either; I never really knew anything different except what I saw when I stayed with my mum at weekends, and I liked what I saw.

Then, in 1994, four years after I'd moved in with

Dad, Rihanna popped into the world. Mum had got together with Rihanna's dad, Ricky, and been really happy, but shortly after Rihanna was born, he passed away. It was a difficult time. So living with Mum were Tony, Nicola and Rihanna, while I lived alone with Dad and Julie, which I found even harder to accept.

I can remember how I felt on those Sunday evenings as I prepared to leave. Nicola and Tony would always be messing around, and Rihanna would be as cute as anything tottering around, while I'd go and pack up my stuff. I hated that time. It made me feel like a visitor and, if I'm honest, really envious of the life they had with my mum. It was such a loud house, filled with a load of kids. I'd watch them mucking around and watching TV, and that Sunday feeling would hit me like a sickness bug every week. Mum's house was just totally different to Dad's. It was crazy and I loved the buzz. She had no rules and it seemed so much fun in comparison. There would be loads of banter between everyone. They were always smiling and laughing and enjoying life. In my mind it was simple – it just didn't seem fair and I wanted to be at Mum's.

Most weekends I would have to catch a bus back to Dad's with Mum, so I had to leave at a certain time, and I could feel myself growing sadder and sadder as the clock neared that time. I longed to stay and be part of the chaos and fun. It didn't help that I shared a bedroom with Nicola, because that made it hard to go back to Dad's too. I loved the company and hated being on my own. I'd always feel so isolated and quite frightened. When I was in Nicola's room, though, I felt at home and comfortable. I adored having them all around me. I felt loved and part of something. I'd feel lonely when I was back at Dad and Julie's in my bedroom all on my own after such a bustling household. Even now I hate being alone.

To be fair on Dad and Julie, I do have lots of happy memories of growing up. When I was about ten, Dad, Julie and I went to Portugal. It was a really lovely holiday and Dad spent hours with me, which I adored. I needed that kind of love and attention; that's the sort of child I was. We went sightseeing or to museums every day, as both Dad and Julie liked to keep busy. I remember one particular day, though, we just went to the beach and Dad built a boat for me out of sand. It was amazing. He was so talented with stuff like that and I'd always wonder how he could rustle up something so realistic so quickly. Dad works with his hands every day and is very creative. That day on the beach is a lovely memory for me. I was really happy and Dad had so much time for me, just me, and I craved that. The bottom line is that I wanted to be loved, and I still do, and on that holiday Dad made sure that I had his undivided attention, and I revelled in it.

My dad is a gentle man and has a massively soft spot for animals. His caring side really rubbed off on me and even now with fluffy animals, I am so soppy it's ridiculous. I had a few animals when I was living with Dad. My first pet was a pure-white rabbit called Snowy. My dad found her hopping down our road and I begged him to let me keep her – she was so cute and I fell in love with her straight away. Dad said I could keep her on one condition – that I looked after her, which meant I would have to clean out her hutch and feed her morning and night, which I obviously agreed to. Dad built a hutch for her and also a run that attached to it. Every day come rain or shine I would be out sitting in the garden playing with Snowy. If Dad couldn't find me, then I'd be in the garden with Snowy – I loved her and she loved me. In fact, every morning I'd go out into the garden in my pyjamas to see her, as Snowy was literally the first thing I thought about when I woke up.

One morning, though, when we'd had Snowy for about four years, I went out into the garden to see her and there was a huge hole in the side of her hutch. Oh my God, I can remember it like it was yesterday. It was awful. I could see a hole in the wire and there was loads of fur strewn all over the lawn. My heart sank. I knew that something bad had happened and I could feel hot tears running down my cheeks as it dawned on me that Snowy was no more. A fox had got in and killed her. I looked everywhere for her, hoping that she was hiding and that the fox had got away without properly hurting her, but I knew in my heart of hearts that she was gone.

I ran into the house sobbing. Dad and Julie were like, 'What's happened? What's wrong?' and in between trying to catch my breath, I told them what I had just seen. Dad went out there straight away, but it wasn't going to bring Snowy back – she had gone. Thank God for small mercies, but I didn't see any blood or anything – I think that would have tipped me over the edge! That was one of the times that I can remember when Dad gave me a hug. He knew how much Snowy meant to me and I think deep down he was gutted too. He cleared it all up so that I didn't have to see it again, but I was distraught. It felt as though I had lost my best friend. I had spent practically every waking hour with her and she had been cruelly ripped away from me. It was awful. There was nothing anyone could do to console me, and no other white rabbit would have replaced her.

After Snowy, I had a few other pets. Dad had a load of fish in the pond, which I used to go outside and enjoy feeding, and I decided I'd like a tank inside of my own, so one birthday I asked for a tropical fish tank. It was huge and full of beautiful fish. I think my dad loved it more than me if truth be told, but it was what I wanted and it was amazing.

Much as I loved it, though, I preferred my cuddles with Snowy. We had several dogs growing up too, and I think they came the closest to matching the affections I had for Snowy. They were a big part of my childhood. We'd often go for family walks over Epping Forest with them. Most days just me and Nan Phyllis, Julie's mum, would take the dogs for a walk. I really enjoyed those times – we took the same route every day and I would sing to Nan all the way round. Dad and I would also often go for walks with the dogs on Sunday afternoons. I can remember evenings when it was getting dark and Dad and I would walk the dogs out over the fields and I could see Canary Wharf and the light flashing on the top of the building. It reminded me of my mum because she lived in Bethnal Green. I used to say, 'Daddy, that's near where Mummy lives.' I missed her so much.

Our dog at that time was a Border collie called Georgie. He was my favourite pet that I ever had and I had him for his whole life. He adored me and I adored him. Nan Phyllis had a mongrel, which was a rescue dog, called Jessie. Jessie was a bit aggressive at first, but

Nan Phyllis managed to train her really well and in the end she was lovely.

Then, a few years later, we got Holly, a boxer dog. She was pure white and I loved her. She was so playful and friendly, and I'd spend hours with her having fun. Not long after we got Holly, though, she got into a fight. I was terrified I was going to lose her like I had Snowy. That was a really horrible evening. I was in the kitchen having a bowl of cornflakes when Julie came through and told me not to go into the front room. She was trying to distract me with anything she could, but I knew something was up. I could see through the door that Holly's white coat was stained with blood and that she was in a real state. My dad was cleaning up Holly's mouth, which was a mess. I had tears running down my face as I saw her whimpering in pain. I really didn't think she would pull through and that night I went to bed thinking Holly wouldn't be there in the morning. She was a fighter, though, and after a few days of TLC from us all, she was back to the bouncing boxer she had been before. Thank God.

Dad loves animals so much he even likes spiders and flies, and he would go mental if I ever killed one. I still don't like insects, though. The other day I had to sleep at my mate Lisa Sourou's house because there was a butterfly in my place and it kept flying at me. I was so scared. It was black with orange bits on and I was proper terrified. There was no way I could sleep there on my own with that thing flying about!

As well as Snowy and the other animals in my life, I had my nannies Jan and Rose. They were always there no matter what. Nanny Jan is my dad's mum. We are very close and I spent lots of time with her growing up. I still do today! She has always spoilt me rotten and we have a very special relationship. Nanny Rose was my dad's nan, and I was her first great-grandchild. As well as my dad, my great-nanny Rose was actually at my birth, on 19 September 1986, in Hackney, London, at Homerton Hospital. My mum wanted her there as they were very close. Because of what happened when I was a child, and because it was a bit unsettling for me, I really looked to my nanny Rose for comfort.

She was a beautiful woman, and Rose is my middle name after her. She was sort of the matriarch of the family, and I have really happy memories of Nanny Rose with her garden full of gnomes! She had a greenhouse at the bottom of the garden where I remember my great-granddad George would spend his days. He passed away when I was much younger, so I don't remember him very well, but my nanny was in my life for a lot longer and played a massive part in my early years.

Nanny Rose was an amazing cook. I can still remember the smell of her cakes baking in the oven and wafting through the house. It makes my mouth water just thinking about it. My favourite was her Victoria sponge with cream and jam. Yum. Nanny Rose spent so much time cooking – I can picture her now in her old-fashioned galley kitchen with its brown wallpaper, baking and then baking some more! I'd spend hours over at hers playing with my cousins, Molly and Maisy, and my second cousins, Nicola and Justine – my aunts on my dad's side. They were good times, and when I think about it, she was the only real constant in my life from day one and she meant the world to me.

I was devastated when she passed away on 2 February 2007 at the age of ninety-seven. It was a good age, but I loved her so much and it was such a hard time for me. I couldn't stand that she'd been taken away when I relied on her and needed her.

Her funeral was the first one I had ever been to and it really affected me. I was twenty when she passed away, and even now when I think about Dad and his mum, Nanny Jan, calling me to tell me that she had gone, it really upsets me. That phone call still haunts me like it was yesterday, and as they said the words, I couldn't take it in. It was like someone had punched me in the stomach. I felt sick knowing I would never see her or be able to talk to her again. It sends a cold shiver down my spine whenever I think about that moment. Oh my God, it truly was awful. She gave me happy memories and helped me cope with some really difficult times, especially when I first went to live with Dad and Julie.

Nanny Rose left such a big gap in my life that I well up just thinking about her not being here. If I'm having a bad day, I will talk to her as if she is still around and can help me. I ask her questions in my head. When I'm confused or not sure what to do, I ask her to put me on the right path. Even though she's not here in body, I know her spirit is around me. She will always have a place in my heart. She had a massive impact on who I am today.

As I got older, the differences between living with Mum and living with Dad felt even more confusing and I started to rebel a bit. It wasn't like I didn't get on with Julie as a child, but as time went on and I started to have a mind of my own, we clashed big time. I recall when I was about seven and she bought a floral dress for me to wear to school. She laid it out on my bed and I remember walking in and seeing it. It had this horrible netting underneath to puff it out. Julie came into the bedroom with me. I think she was really excited that she had got it for me, but I hated it immediately. It was awful. I feel bad now because Julie would always spend quite a lot of money on clothes for me, but the dress was ugly and the idea of me wearing it was unthinkable! I turned to her and I was like, 'I'm not wearing that. No way.' She said, 'Lauren, just try it on and see what you think,' but I refused even to do that and she wasn't happy at all. It really mugged her off. She just walked out of my bedroom and told me to wear what I liked. She had the right hump, which I suppose is understandable.

When I started to get a bit of a voice for myself, our relationship seemed to decline. It wasn't often that I argued or said what I thought, because I didn't ever want any trouble. I never wanted to upset anyone and I hated being told off. I wanted everyone to be happy. I didn't like rows and upset, and I still don't. I want the quiet life in that sense. I suppose with Julie and me, a part of me resented her because she wasn't my mum, but was still trying to be that motherly figure to me. There's no doubt in my mind that she did really care for me, but her and Dad's strict rules were hard going when Mum didn't have any at all, and that's a big deal for a child.

Things improved for me when Tony and Nicola got a bit older – I think they were about eight and ten – and they started to come and stay with me at my dad's for weekends. I loved having them stay and I'd get so excited on a Friday knowing they were coming over. It's funny because they seemed envious of the life I led with Dad. They saw the great birthday parties I had. There was one when Dad hired out a swimming pool and we had slides and this massive blow-up octopus that went on top of the water. It was every kid's dream party! They also hired halls for my parties, and we had barbecues some years in the garden. As I got older, Dad would pay for me and my friends to go to Chessington World of Adventures or Alton Towers, and then everyone would come back to mine for a sleepover.

Tony and Nicola also saw the holidays Dad took me on. We'd go all over the place – like Lanzarote, Turkey and Spain – and I think they wanted to be part of that and to go on holiday too. They didn't get to go away with Mum as much, so it seemed exciting and an adventure. I think they thought I was really spoiled, but all I wanted was my mum and dad's love and attention, and if they really knew how I felt, they would have known that I would have rather have gone away with Mum and them. They envied me and I envied them. I did have good holidays with Dad, but they were always very active and we would sightsee, go on boats and climb mountains. We would always be doing something. It had to be very cultural 'cos that's how my dad and Julie liked it. There was never really an opportunity to relax and sunbathe like I wanted to because we were constantly on the go.

I only went on holiday with my mum once and that was about three years ago when we went to Tenerife. As you can imagine, it was a very different experience. It was chilled and relaxed, and we sunbathed round the pool every day, which is what I like doing. I didn't like doing things at a hundred miles an hour. I wasn't bothered about museums and sightseeing and all that stuff, and Mum got that – probably because she didn't like it much either.

The more weekends that Tony and Nicola spent with us, the closer they became to Dad and Julie, and Nicola was even a bridesmaid at their wedding, in 1991. They became so close that Nicola started calling my dad 'Dad'. I can remember when she first did it. It was so weird. We were in Epping Forest and she was on this bridge and she called out, 'Dad.' She had heard me calling him 'Dad' and had copied. She didn't have her dad around, so she wanted to be like me. I was OK with it, and so was Dad. For me, the weekends that they came felt really good. It was a very full house with us all there together and it made me happy. For once I didn't feel lonely.

When I was ten, though, after six years living with Dad, there was a big change for me when Dad and Julie started their own family. I was so excited. I couldn't wait to have a baby brother or sister for me to love and take care of. Then Hayley was born and she was adorable. She had dark hair and brown eyes. I was so happy to have a little sister. I'd try and do everything for her, like change her nappy and cuddle and kiss her. She made me happy.

Then, eleven months later, Julie fell pregnant again and gave birth to another girl, called Jenna. Jenna was just as cute as Hayley except she was the complete opposite: she had blonde hair and blue eyes. The house felt suddenly full with two babies and a bit more complete. In some ways when I look back, there was a part of me that was envious, I think, because they had a proper family with a mum and dad who loved each other and lived together. My family was all over the place and I suppose I did feel a bit left out. That was no fault of Julie or my dad; it's just how I felt.

Dad did his best – I can't knock him or Julie for that. He would always make time for me. I was his little girl, and when he came in from work, he'd spend ages in my bedroom with me and we would chat about all sorts of things. He'd say to me, 'Anything you want to talk about, Lauren?' He'd ask me if there was anything worrying me and we would discuss my future. Dad always wanted me to do something with my life. At times I felt suffocated by that and as though I couldn't be me, but I know that he and Julie had good intentions.

My dad had a thing about me turning out like my mum. He worried that I'd end up like her, and he thought I wasn't going to get a good job, so he tried everything possible to make me academic and have a life that he wanted for me. Their idea of me knuckling down and studying was clearly not happening, though. I was more interested in fashion and make-up and going out with my mates, and no matter how hard they pushed, I knew I was never gonna be the girl who became a doctor or a lawyer. Dad and Julie wanted so much for me and wanted me to be something I was never gonna be. I was never gonna go to uni – I was always gonna let them down on that front. Mum couldn't understand it at all, but that's the way they were, and as I have got older, I can appreciate why they did what they did. I know they just wanted the best for me. At the time, though, it was weird because I felt like Dad didn't know who I was, that he didn't understand me. It was as if he wanted me to be something I wasn't.

Dad is proud of me now, but he tried his best to get me into something steady. It just didn't work, and I could have told him that at the time.

As I got older and became more and more aware of how different it was to be at my mum's, the more unfair I thought it was and the more I wanted to move back in with her. All I wanted was to be with my friends and have a good time. I'm a party girl at heart and love to have a good time. Even at that age I wanted and craved fun in my life. I wanted to play with my friends rather than learning to play an instrument. I remember when I was about twelve and Dad, Julie and I were having dinner one night and I told them I didn't want to be in the netball team any more. I was fed up of having to do so many activities outside school. I was like, 'I'm gonna quit netball. I don't like it,' and Julie was mad. She didn't want me to jack it in. She wanted me to stick with it. Dad was the same in a way. They wanted to keep me focused. They were early birds and would always be up early doing stuff and they'd like me up and about too, which I loathed. I hated mornings, and still do, and I'd find it really hard to get up. Dad was very hands-on and would be the one every day to come in and get me up for school. He used to bring me a cup of tea and two shortcake biscuits without fail every morning. Even if I said I didn't want them, he'd bring them in anyway.

You'll laugh at this, but when I went over to my mum's at weekends, I was really aware that I spoke posh in comparison to them. Seriously. I'm not joking, but in the end I actually taught myself to speak with a cockney accent because I didn't wanna be the posh one and the odd one out. How mad is that? It's ridiculous. I hated being little Miss Posh. In my head it just made me even less a part of the family I wanted to be with and was so envious of when I went home on a Sunday night. I hated feeling different. I wanted to be cool like them even if I wasn't allowed to live there. I thought I was really cool when my sister Nicola bought me a mobile phone. Nicola had come on the bus to pick me up for the weekend, which she sometimes did, and had brought it for me as a surprise so that I could be in contact with them all the time. I was only twelve and I thought I was 'it', but Dad went ballistic. Proper ballistic. I didn't care. I was like the cat that had got the cream with my Nokia and thought it was the best thing in the world being able to speak to Mum whenever I wanted. But every time I did something I wasn't supposed to do, it was the first thing to be taken off me. It really got to me because that was my independence and my direct line to my other family. It was the worst punishment and I hated Dad if he took it away.

My parents have always remained civil for my sake, but they don't speak unless they have to, and when I was a kid, although I tried not to get involved, they would say the odd thing about each other to me. For instance, it used to really annoy Mum that Julie would cut my hair short. Mum knew I wanted to have it long, but every four weeks I'd have it cut. I even had a fringe cut in, which Mum hated, and she would say to me, 'Why does she keep doing that? For God's sake, I wish they'd stop cutting your hair.' I hated it too. I was desperate for long hair like my friends, but on the plus side, it was in good nick – no split ends! Mum would blame Dad for not standing up to Julie and would say he was weak, but I would never repeat what they said about each other because I didn't want to get involved. These days Mum and Dad get along if they have to see each other, like at my birthday parties or at work dos, but I'd hardly call them the best of friends!

Whenever I was with Mum, Dad would always be calling and checking up on me. I don't have many memories of how Mum and Dad were with each other, and I don't specifically remember them arguing, but I do remember him calling all the time. I think she felt as though he didn't trust her with me and that used to upset her. I can remember one specific incident when I went up to London with Mum. It was New Year's

Eve and he kept calling me to see if I was OK. He wanted me at home because he had loads of family round and I don't think he could understand why I'd rather be in town with my mum. His calls really hacked her off. It made her feel as though he thought she was incapable of looking after me and it mugged her off. Nanny Jan said he only did it because he cared so much about me and worried for me, but I was OK – I was with Mum.

Like any ex-wife and new wife, Mum and Julie have never seen eye to eye or got on very well. I never really knew what was going on or what was being said, but Julie didn't seem to like my mum and she would sometimes say stuff about her, which my dad stopped her doing because he could see that it upset me so much. I think I came first when it came to my dad's affections in the early days, and if ever there was a row, he would always take my side and that must have got to Julie at times. He couldn't see any wrong in me and that probably used to piss off Julie! Mum didn't see that and she used to get annoyed at Dad because she thought he was weak for agreeing to do everything that Julie wanted and so it went on.

It's weird really because Mum, Dad and Julie only wanted what was best and for me to be happy. I was actually loved by everyone, yet so much of the time I felt caught in the middle and lost as a person. It all started to build up to the point where I couldn't take any more.

For a long time I'd known that I wanted to leave Dad's and move in with Mum, but I was too scared to say anything to my dad and never had the courage to do anything about it. I would often try and stay with my mum once the weekend was over. She would ask me to go back and live with her, but my dad would always say no and would make me go back home. I never talked to Dad properly about my feelings. Mum kept saying to me, 'Just tell him you want to come and live with me,' but I didn't want to get in trouble, so I thought the easiest thing was to run away. It sounds crazy writing that now, but I guess I was young and impulsive. I loved my little sisters Jenna and Hayley, but when I was becoming a teenager and they were just two and three, I desperately wanted to be back with Tony and Nicola, who were closer in age to me. Rihanna was still a kid, but Nicola I looked up to so much.

I was thirteen when I finally plucked up the courage to run away. I'd been toying with the idea and then one day something just snapped inside me and I decided to go for it. I'd had enough and wanted to be part of the life Tony and Nicola were leading. I hadn't told anyone what I was going to do, although I knew that Mum wanted me back to live with her, so I knew she would be happy. On the day itself I was so nervous that I was shaking. I really quickly threw a mixture of clothes in a holdall because I didn't want to be caught packing. I didn't take any of the rest of the stuff from my room; I left it there and that's where it stayed. I wanted to get away without anyone noticing, which was a total cop-out, but I didn't want any trouble. And that was it – I caught the bus on my own, which was scary in itself, and started my one-way journey to my mum's.

I think my dad has never really forgiven me and now I'm an adult I can understand why he was so upset. He was probably frantic when he realised I'd gone, or perhaps deep down he knew where I was. I think he knew I wanted to be with my mum again. I'm not sure who he spoke to – maybe it was my mum – but from what I remember I didn't speak to him about it. I know that I didn't face the consequences head on, and me legging it caused a lot of problems. It took him ages to accept that I was gone and not coming back.

Dad and Julie had only just moved to Loughton from our previous house in Redbridge, not too far from my mum's place, but apart from the odd weekend I didn't visit much after that for a few reasons – mainly, I think, because he really struggled with my decision. After all,

I had chosen to live with my mum and my dad was gutted. He was upset and couldn't understand why I'd wanted to go. I couldn't explain why it was so important to me to be back with my mum. Running away is probably the scariest thing I've ever done. I was terrified and I know I really hurt my dad in doing it. Tony, my brother, is always telling me how much Dad used to do for me, and how if there was a row between me and Julie, he would stand up for me, and I do feel bad – he only wanted what was best for me. My nanny Jan, my dad's mum, tells me that all the time.

I'm sorry to say that my relationship with Dad was never the same again and I don't see him much these days. We speak now and again on the phone, and when we do speak we have a proper catch up and he always tells me he's proud of me. We see each other occasionally. He will turn up to my work events with Hayley and Jenna, and at my twenty-sixth birthday last year he came along, but we aren't close any more.

Julie and I have pretty much lost contact altogether, as I have with Julie's mum, Phyllis, and that makes me really sad. I loved Phyllis and she was always so kind to me. I haven't spoken to her or Julie in ages, and I can't see that changing now – it would be too awkward. I think too much time has passed and I'm not sure what we'd say to one another. I suppose we have grown apart to the point where we don't even speak. I suspect there is a part of her that finds it hard to accept that I ran away after everything she did for me, and now I am older, I get that. She did do so much for me, and I have a lot to thank her for, but when I ran away, I was a child. I wanted my mum and my older brother and sister around me. I don't blame her if she did feel upset by what I did.

I really did care for Julie, but it was always up and down. I felt as though one minute she was OK with me, and the next she would blow cold. I suppose running away was like a big fat slap in the face. It didn't help the way I did it. I literally packed a bag, got on a bus, met my mum and never went back.

As my little sisters Hayley and Jenna have got older, we have become really close. Jenna is fifteen now and Hayley is sixteen, and we do talk about our childhoods. Not much – I think we all look forward rather than back – but they have asked me a few things, like why I decided to leave, and when they were younger, they asked why I didn't live with them any more. It was weird for them and they missed me. We used to all watch films together and I'd make them laugh and suddenly I wasn't there any longer, which was confusing for them. They didn't really understand what had happened. Even now they text or call me every day to say they love me and miss me. They are great girls and so proud of me and what I've achieved. They will often call me and I'll have to speak to their friends to prove that I really am their sister because we don't share the same surname – I have my mother's surname, while my dad's is Norman – and their friends don't believe them! It's hilarious. Dad and Julie are quite different with Hayley and Jenna than they were with me, I think. They aren't nearly as strict and the girls are allowed tellies in their room! I don't know why, but they seem to be way more relaxed with them. I see myself as lucky because I have four siblings and despite the set up we, until recently, have been really close. Even when Tony and Nicola didn't come to my dad's anymore they were a massive part of my life and I'm really grateful for that.

Looking back, I can see I was impulsive and naïve to run away. Inevitably, moving back to my mum's wasn't quite what I thought it would be. I thought it would be the answer to making me happy finally, but it wasn't. I turned up and straight away it wasn't quite what I had hoped. I went to Nicola's room with my holdall and unpacked my assortment of possessions. It was a bit like going on holiday and loving it and then going there to live and it not being quite as good. Does that make sense? That's kind of how I felt that first night. I didn't question what I'd done, but I wanted it to be so much more – I wanted to feel fulfilled. I'd always felt like something was missing, so it was a shock to realise that night that I still felt that way. That warm, glowy feeling that I thought I'd have wasn't there, and as each day passed, I found it increasingly hard to settle.

After all those years away, building a relationship with Mum wasn't easy. Most kids have always lived with their mum and I hadn't. We had to get to know one another again, which was really hard. Readjusting to Mum's parenting style took a while to get used to, after living with Dad for so long. All that I really wanted was to have a mum and that's why I wanted to move back, but when I had moved back, I still wasn't satisfied, which made me question what I really wanted. Perhaps I didn't know.

Mum and I didn't always get on, and I felt like I was the problem, as though I was at fault. It was like I was an outsider, and although I loved her, I wanted her to be more of a mum to me. I wanted to depend on her, rather than the other way round. Mum suffers from depression and anxiety, and in my opinion that really affected her being a mum to me. She has a good side and a bad side. She can be funny, but she can also be quite difficult. No matter how hard we tried, I don't think we could have got a proper mother–daughter relationship back again. We haven't given up trying though and we have just started to go shopping together and doing stuff again which is really nice. I hope that continues because I do love her. There was a distance between us but I want so much for that to change. At one stage it felt like we were growing further and further apart but now it's going the other way and I am so pleased.

I do think what happens to you when you are growing up shapes you as a human being. I'm sure my unconventional childhood has played a big part in the insecurities I have now. I don't blame anyone and that's genuine. My mum has been through a lot in her life and I know that she must have really believed that it was best for me to live with Dad. It's not my place to start going into her business and talking about her life, but what I will say is that it's been difficult for her. So when I question her actions, I remind myself of that. I don't think I feel resentment, but, like I say, I'm sure that her decision had a huge effect on me and has played a big part in who I am today.

I had craved for so long to have a warm family around me, but the life I thought I wanted didn't shape up to be what I expected. Mum felt that I resented her for giving me to my dad, even though I have never said that. She thought I questioned whether she really wanted me or not, but I don't think I did, at least not consciously.

Sharing a room with Nicola was fun at the weekends, but I'd been used to having a room all to myself, and when it became normal, I did wish I had a bit more space. Suddenly living with siblings close in age to me was hard, which I hadn't expected. We had never all lived together, just weekends, and at times we clashed – there were a lot of hormones in one place! I felt lost and a bit empty, kind of confused.

Nicola started to go out more with her friends and would be out of the house on Friday and Saturday nights. I desperately wanted to be out with her, but I just wasn't old enough. Each week I would hope that she would stay in and her mates would come round so that I wouldn't be on my own. When I was at an age I could go out, there would be murders in the house as we nicked each other's outfits and make-up. We'd really wind each other up.

While Mum and I had to start from the beginning again as mother and daughter, I also battled with the guilt of leaving my dad. The older and more mature I became, the more guilty I felt. When I look back, I think I had real courage to leave, but the way I did it was wrong. I was only young and it was probably the hardest decision I had ever made.

I feel like I've given Dad and Julie a hard time, because they really did try, in their own way, to do their best for me. Even without their strict rules I was never going to be truly happy. Julie was a good step-mum and tried hard. She would take me up to London and spend £100 on a dress for me and the nicest shoes. That was a lot of money in those days. She'd send me to school with the best packed lunches and every one of my classmates would be jealous. There wasn't one sports day or performance at theatre school that she or Dad missed. They were so supportive and always encouraged me to fufil my potential.

I wasn't lying when I said my family was confusing, was I? I'm not gonna start blaming my childhood, but it has made me who I am today. I know I can't regret something I had no say in, but I do wish things could have been different. I was very lost as a child and I was looking for something, but I wasn't sure what. It's not surprising that when Mark came along at the age of fifteen, he became my main focus. He was my escape. I wanted a family unit around me. I wanted to be loved and wanted to be part of something, and I thought he and his family offered that.

As I have got older, I have had to try and deal with my insecurities. I'm not very good at showing emotion and I'll try and mask how I'm really feeling. As I said earlier, I find it hard to open up about all of this and admit that my childhood wasn't the happiest of times for me. Instead if I'm ever feeling low, I slap on the make-up, put on a dress, team it with a good handbag and a pair of Louboutins, and hit the town with a smile on my face. Underneath it all, though, that's not me. I like a good night out, but I'd swap it tomorrow for marriage and a family. I want to feel that security and have a family that isn't all fractured. I want my kids to have a mum and dad who love each other, where the kids come top of the list. I want my kids to have a happy childhood – that's all I really want. My early years have made me determined to have a marriage that works and to love my children more than anything in the world. That's what is really important to me. I'd give it all up tomorrow for that.

2

Fake Tan + Make-up + Blow-dry = AMAZING

THANK YOU FOR USING
NORFOLK LIBRARIES
You can renew items online,
by Spydus Mobile Phone App
or by phone at 0344 800 8020
Ask staff about email alerts
before books become overdue

Self Service Receipt for Check Out

Name: **********2373

Title: Secrets of an Essex girl /
[hardback]

Item: 30129069983071

Due Back: 31/12/2021

Total Check Out: 1
10/12/2021 10:20:34

Norfolk Library and Information Service
Please keep your receipt

IT'S TRUE – YOU take those ingredients and however low you are feeling, you will immediately feel better. Fact. Team them with some decent clothes and you're ready to take on the world. I *love* fashion and make-up, and always have done.

As a very self-aware child, these things played a big part in making me feel good about myself. It's only recently that I've recognised that I battled quite a few insecurities from a very young age. Some I am now learning to deal with, and some I don't think will ever fully go away. I will go into more detail later in the book about those battles, but right now I want to concentrate on my more light-hearted obsession with make-up and clothes, and at one stage a very real addiction to being tanned! I am not joking.

Looking my best has always been important to me. I love the glamour of celebs like J Lo, Kim Kardashian and Beyoncé. They always look totally polished and amazing, and when I was a kid I'd spend a massive amount of time trying to look like them. I'd go into the bathroom looking like one person and then a few hours later come out looking like another! I wanted to look perfect wherever I was going. Even if it was for a pint of milk down the shop with my mum, I would make sure I had my make-up on. If I went shopping with my mates, I'd spend at least two hours getting myself ready and doing my hair. It was like a hobby to me – trying out new looks and practising different make-up techniques. I suppose I was vain, but not in the sense that I would stare at myself as I walked past a mirror. I just couldn't stand the idea of not looking my best all the time. I wanted to make myself feel like a star every day, and I did. When I was shopping down the high road with my mates, it would be . . . Hair? Check. Make-up? Check. Fake tan? Check. I was at my happiest and I loved it.

I was always rebellious when it came to the way I wanted to look. When I was younger and still living at my dad's, I wasn't allowed to wear make-up, but I wasn't prepared to just roll over and not wear any. Instead at the weekends I'd get my fix when I went to visit Mum. I'd go and sit in her room for hours trying on all of hers. Nicola would

44

often come in and keep me company, showing me how to wear mascara and apply foundation. I'd watch her apply it and then try it myself. I'd practise and practise until I got the look I was after just right. I never really had the kind of relationship with Mum where she sat with me and showed me how to put on make-up; it wasn't like that between us. Nicola did a pretty good job of showing me what to do, though, and I hung on her every word!

It wasn't just Dad and Julie who were anti me wearing make-up; my school, Roden Valley, in Loughton, wasn't keen on it either and pupils weren't supposed to wear any. Those were the rules, but I didn't care – there was no way I was gonna rock up at the gates with a bare face. No way! So on school days I would set my alarm and get up early to wash and blow-dry my hair. Then when I'd left the house and was out of sight, I'd hide round the corner and apply my make-up. Then it was the same drill in reverse on the way back. I'd hide and remove the make-up before going into the house so they never knew I'd been wearing any. #sneaky

I did the same with my clothes. I think most girls have done it at some point or other, but I'd leave the house with my skirt at an acceptable length and then when I got out the door, I'd roll it up so that it was really short. I'd have a pair of high heels in my bag and I'd change into them to complete the look.

I didn't have to worry about hiding how I was dressing at Mum's – she would let me wear short skirts and heels – but I rarely went from her house to school, so I'd have to do the whole secret change most days. I became very good at it, and I still don't think Dad and Julie ever knew I did it! They would have been horrified if they'd known what I got up to.

I loved school. I can honestly say that now, although at the time I'd have said something very different. I moaned about it constantly, and I didn't like all the lessons and that, but now I'm older and having to work, I realise how good those times really were. They were happy days and I felt part of something with my group of friends; for the first time I felt mostly at ease and comfortable and in control. I was always part of the cool group and was able to be me with no one trying to turn me into something I wasn't. I led the pack rather than followed, and I was a very different person to the child I was at home. I did clash with some of the teachers – mainly over the make-up I'd wear into school or my take on the school uniform. They told me that I looked like I was at a fashion parade because I was so dolled up. I took that as a compliment! Lol.

Most of my pocket money went on make-up and my other love – clothes. I wanted to follow the fashion and be the one to be wearing the latest trends. Probably like most people, I thought at the time that I looked great, but when I look at some of the pictures now, there were some embarrassing outfits. Like the awful shiny black bomber jacket with the horrible orange lining I wore. You know that early 1990s look? Everyone had one, but they were so gross. Seriously, I wore some really chavvy outfits that I'd rather forget about, but I thought I was really cool. I didn't seem to realise that nothing ever matched! I can remember buying some white platform trainers like the Spice Girls wore. I wanted to be a Spice Girl, so when I saw them in Dolcis or Barratts, I had to have a pair! My dad wouldn't let me wear them because he thought they were too high, so I hid them in the back of my wardrobe and then if I wanted to wear them, I'd sneak them out of the house and change once I'd been dropped off or was far enough away for no one to see. I bought a pair for my friend as well and her parents banned them, so they too got stashed at the back of my bedroom wardrobe for when the parents weren't about! Most embarrassing has to be the all-gold sovereign ring I had. I feel sick thinking about it. Can you believe I wore one? Ugh. I can't believe I actually wore it and liked it and thought it was cool. Ridiculous. Dad bought me a gold chain with my initials on, but even that now is a bit chavvy, isn't it? Really, there I was loving fashion and desperate to be cool wearing that kind of crap. I didn't have a clue.

It wasn't just clothes that I experimented with; my hair copped it too. I went through a phase of spraying Sun-In in my hair, but it went completely wrong and instead of having nice blonde highlighted streaks, it went orange. People were like, 'What the hell have you done? Stop getting bored and dying it.' I looked awful and at that age there wasn't really much I could do about it – I had to live with ridiculous-looking hair and the jibes until it faded. I hated it, but it didn't stop me dyeing it again. I even went through a phase of having it almost black. I was always changing the colour of my hair.

I had clip-in hair extensions for a while too. I bought £40 clip-ins from the afro stall at Walthamstow Market. I saw them one day while I was out with my mates shopping and I couldn't wait to get them home to put them in. I loved them – they made my hair look instantly fuller and more styled. I was the first person out of my mates to wear anything like that and they all wanted some. Then I saw that a few shops at Lakeside were selling really realistic clip-in extensions, so I saved up and bought myself them too. They were £150, which was a lot, but I had to have them and was really good at saving birthday and Christmas money. If I went out with my mates, I'd spend hours putting them in and they gave me my first taste of what extensions were all about.

I spent years experimenting and finding out what I

did and didn't like, and although I hate a lot of the pictures of me, my passion and interest in beauty and fashion were obvious. From a very young age I chose to go shopping with my mates rather than watch TV or do a hobby like other kids at school. We'd catch the bus and go to Lakeside Shopping Centre in West Thurrock. It was only about half an hour from my mum's house and about forty minutes from my dad's, and it was something I looked forward to all week. Mostly we'd spend the day wandering around all the shops, but when I had some money on me, I'd go to TK Maxx because I could get really cool branded stuff at bargain prices. I'd also buy clothes from trendy high-street stores like Bay Trading and River Island. Apart from partying, shopping is still my favourite hobby and I'll often go to Lakeside for my fix, although it's not quite so easy to get around now! Shopping is something I will never get bored of. I'm a typical girly girl.

My clothes caused a fair bit of trouble between myself and my step-mum, Julie – like the flowery dress we didn't see eye to eye on. I don't think she realised that if I'd worn that, I'd have been bullied! Even at seven years old, I knew that I didn't want to wear it. She had her ideas about what I should be wearing, and I had mine. I don't think she ever liked my concept of fashion and we would have loads of rows about it, but it was one thing I wouldn't have my mind changed on. It was probably the only thing, in fact, that I would stand up for myself about and try and get my own way with. It was my outlet and my passion. Mum would encourage me – she hated what Julie tried to dress me in and would be like, 'What the hell are you wearing?' when I turned up there on weekends. I would love the clothes Nicola wore, so she would let me get changed into a nice pair of her jeans, a top and some boots.

I think boys are attracted to girls who have spent a bit of time on themselves, as in wearing nice clothes or applying make-up. Although I was only a kid really when I met Mark, having a boyfriend meant that looking good was even more important to me if that's possible. There are days now when I like to sit at home in my tracksuit bums and relax with no make-up on and my hair tied back, but when I was a kid I'd never really have those days. I wanted to look good, and putting my make-up on and getting dressed up was all part of my day. It was fun.

It was around that time that I also started to get addicted to being brown! I loathed looking pasty and still do. I was only fifteen when I started going on sun beds. I'd use them two or three times a week for about twelve-minute sessions each time. I knew they weren't good for me, but I didn't care – I was obsessed with

Cute baby pic!

Learning to
swim with
my stepmum
Julie

I've always
had a passion
for fashion!

Here I am with the Dulux dog!

Giving Picasso a run for his money

Here I am with my granddad

Pretty in pink as a bridesmaid at my dad's wedding

Christmas has always been one of my favourite times of year

Splashing around with Dad!

Chats before bedtime

Grown up, glammed up!

Me and Mark with baby Wrighty

Mark and I at a charity football match. We did have some good times

Have to say we did look good together

Celebrating my engagement. I meant it when I said forever

Sparkling at
the BAFTAS

Amy, Lydia, Sam and me at the BAFTAS

looking tanned. I wanted to look as though I had been on a two-week holiday to Marbs every day of the year. As soon as the sun was out, I was in the back garden covered in oil trying to catch a tan. No lie, it became like an addiction, and when I moved on from sun beds, I started to apply fake tan every single day. Seriously, I was a tanaholic! I thought I looked great, until Nicola and my mum said to me that I looked a bit ridiculous. I didn't listen to them because I liked the way I looked and it made me feel confident, but I was this weird shade of mahogany!

My extreme tanning didn't last for long because I was always trying to reinvent myself and I started to panic about my skin ageing, about the damage I was doing to it and about it becoming wrinkly. You'll find this really hard to believe, but at one stage when I was about seventeen years old I decided I wanted to look pale. (It makes me feel sick to think about it now!) I stopped using sun beds and fake tan completely. It was one way to stand out from the crowd because where I'm from, being pale wasn't and isn't in vogue. It didn't last for long obviously. I think it was about a month before I whacked the fake tan back on. I didn't feel human being so pale – I'd catch a glimpse of myself in the mirror and I'd look half dead I was so white.

Fake tan still clearly plays a big part in my life and

I have to pinch myself when I think that I have my own range of tanning products. I don't apply fake tan every day, but I top it up when it needs it and I make sure that I apply it before a night out. I want to look good, but less is more sometimes and I think it's only very recently that I have started to become more comfortable in my own skin and feel as though I don't need to hide behind the tan and the make-up quite as much. I'm still obsessed, but it's a much healthier obsession these days. Don't think you'll catch me anytime soon without a tan or make-up, though – that's not gonna happen!

Strangely, when I was with Mark, I didn't worry too much about him seeing me bare-faced in the mornings. I imagine people expect me to have had a full face of make-up on all the time around him. Like I'd set my alarm early and rush to the bathroom to apply it before he woke up. That honestly couldn't be further from the truth, though. I was with Mark from such a young age that he has seen me at my best and my worst. He would always say to me that I looked the same to him and that made me feel confident. If he was around me, I felt sexy and attractive. That's not to say that I would happily walk out in public with him without any make-up on – I wouldn't.

Now we aren't together any more and I'm on the

dating scene again, I have to battle with myself not to go back to what I know, my default setting of hiding behind it all, but I think I'm winning. On a personal level, I am moving in the right direction and each day I feel like I'm learning to like myself a bit more and I'm trying not to put so much pressure on myself to look a certain way.

Having said that, I do take a full bag of make-up out with me everywhere I go – I don't feel right without it! I don't like the idea of needing it and not having it with me. It's like a security blanket and I feel panicky if I don't have it. If I'm feeling crap, then the make-up goes on and I instantly feel better about myself.

Also, with paparazzi round every corner, the last thing I want is for a picture of me looking rough to turn up in a magazine or newspaper. I have nightmares that they'll get a picture of me with no make-up on and a massive spot on show or something. Those 'caught unaware' shots are always the worst, and when I see myself like that, it makes me feel rubbish.

My trusty favourites that come everywhere with me are my Mac Studio Foundation FC NC30 – a number I know off by heart! Even when you're hanging after a night out on the town, it goes a long way to making you look human again. Bronzer is a big favourite of mine too and I've always got some in my make-up bag. The one I really like isn't even a proper make – it's off the Romford Market and costs me £2! I've used it since I was sixteen and I swear by it. I have tried so hard to find out who makes it to see whether I can buy the rights to it so I can produce it under my business, Lauren's Way, but I've had no luck. I buy it in bulk, in case for any reason they stop selling it down the market. Then, for a bit of colour, I always carry some blusher – Mac 'Breezy Shimmer'. I'm not very keen on matt cheeks and this one gives my cheeks a nice sheen. I get a lot of people writing to me to tell me that they like how I do my make-up and that's a real confidence boost. Here's one letter I received recently:

Dear Lauren Goodger,

My name is Beth. I am from Chelmsford, Essex. I think you are very pretty!

You are my favourite girl on TOWIE. I came to your salon in May for my sixteenth birthday and had a really nice time. I think you are amazing. I am going to study beauty after my GCSEs so I can be like you and one day own my own salon.

Lots of love,

X Beth X

I have been asked several times to pose without any make-up on for magazine shoots and I always feel very nervous about agreeing to do them. I did do one for *Heat* and I was totally make-up-free, but when I saw it, I absolutely hated it. I was completely pared back, and unlike other celebrities who had gone make-up-free before, I thought I looked awful. I hated seeing myself looking pale and as though I hadn't bothered. I had loads of messages from fans saying that they thought I looked great, which was really sweet, but I'm always very critical of myself and it made me feel embarrassed. Anyway, I'm gonna blame my knackered look on Mark because he had turned up at my house the night before the shoot begging me to speak to him. We had split up at that point, back in 2011, but no matter how much I ignored him and how many times I told him to go away, he refused. I eventually let him in and we ended up spending the night together. He talked to me all night about things – us, our future, not wanting us to break up – and by the time my alarm went off at 7 a.m., I was so exhausted I felt sick. The pictures weren't very forgiving, and no matter how many people said I looked good in them, I didn't believe them. It's times like that when my insecurities kick in and I start hating myself. That's what I'm like – I want to look my best all the time, and in my opinion in those pictures I didn't.

In a weird way I felt as though I had let myself down.

Like I said, most of the comments and messages I received were supportive, but as usual there were the odd ones that laid into me. I see these kinds of vile comments on Twitter from people all the time, and even though most days I ignore them, there are days when they can get me down. To tell you the truth, it mugs me off that some people think it's OK to slag me off like that. People can be really cruel when they want to be. They don't even know me, yet they sit there and judge me, and I find that really odd. I'd like to see what they look like!

What's in My Make-up Bag

Mac Studio Foundation FC NC30

Mascara Horn and Lash by Mac in black

Blusher in 'Breezy Shimmer' by Mac

Bronzer from Romford Market! £2 – no make

Eye shadow – Mac palette of browns, golds, silvers and bronzes

Gel eyeliner – Mac

Brows – HD palette

Cherry Carmex lip balm

How to Apply Fake Eyelashes Lauren's Way

I used to wear false eyelashes all the time, not just on nights out. In the second series of *The Only Way Is Essex* I chose to be filmed pretty much constantly with them on. I don't wear them as much any more for two reasons. Firstly, I worry about the damage they will do to my own eyelashes. My lashes are in good condition at the moment and I don't want to ruin them. Someone like Sam Faiers wears them a lot because she suffers from trichotillomania, which means she pulls out her natural eyelashes, and I'm lucky enough to have my own, so I don't want to ruin them by permanently wearing fake lashes. I don't wanna become a slave to having to wear them permanently. Secondly, I have gone off the look of very heavy eyelashes and I try to wear more mascara instead. I occasionally have the individual lashes put on, which I love because they are so natural-looking, but you have to keep having them done, which is costly and would eventually damage your natural eyelashes. On a night out, though, there is no doubt that they add glamour and really set off your eye make-up.

Step 1: Buy a good eyelash glue. Mac Duo adhesive is the best.

Step 2: Put a blob on the back of your hand and let it get tacky for a minute or so.

Step 3: Using your forefinger and thumb, sweep up the glue on to the eyelash.

Step 4: Close one eye and push the lash down from one corner of the eye to the other. (Some people use tweezers, but I prefer a cotton bud.)

Step 5: Finish by putting a line of Mac gel eyeliner over the top so you can't see any joins. To create a seamless look, put some mascara on to join your eyelashes to the fake ones.

How to Apply the Perfect Fake Tan

First, use Lauren's Way products, obvs! Exfoliation is key. I use a Lauren's Way exfoliator. I keep an exfoliation glove and an exfoliation cloth (which I prefer) in the bath and shower, and use either of them to get rid of all the dead skin so the tan goes on smoothly. Apply the tan with a mitt (I use my Lauren's Way one) using circular motions and ensuring that every part of your body is covered. Once it's applied, moisturise regularly.

My Daily Beauty Regime

You probably think I sleep with slices of cucumber on my eyes every night and all that nonsense, after everything I have said about wanting to look my best, but I don't. I actually do very little. Having said that, there are some musts for everyone!

Moisturise every day. Don't forget your neck – you want to keep those wrinkles away! Your neck is always a giveaway of your age. You mustn't put your make-up on until you have moisturised. There is one secret I'll let you in to: if you find a spot, whack a bit of Sudocrem on it. It's genius stuff and always sees them off!

I think the biggest treat you can give your face is a facial whenever you can – I try and have one at least once a fortnight. They cleanse and refresh your skin, and you feel amazing afterwards. You might get a few spots at first, but that's just your skin ridding itself of toxins that have come to the surface and they'll soon go. In the long run, the cleaner your face, the less spots you are likely to get.

Don't forget to remove *all* of your make-up every night, no matter how heavy the night was. If you don't, you'll be covered in spots in no time. I use face wipes to get off my make-up after a heavy night. I use all different brands – Nivea, Simple, Johnson's. On the nights that I have more time, I like to cleanse and tone properly. I *love* Clinique's mousse cleanser because it really foams up, but I also like Dermalogica and Elemis cleansers. Then dab on a bit of toner (I don't have a favourite) and finish with moisturiser. I particularly like the YSL renewal night serum called 'Top Secrets Beauty Sleep Serum' because it really brightens up my skin.

How to Look Your Best on a Night Out

For the first time in eleven years I am single and I am making up for lost time! I'm out most nights and I'm starting to enjoy male attention, and to be truthful I'm having a great time. My life has become hectic and manic with work, but I still love nothing more than having those girly evenings getting ready to go on a big night out. Like everyone, I expect, I have a bit of a 'going out' routine, but for me, getting ready is all part of the fun. There'll always be a few us getting ready, so I'll put on some R&B or funky house or Rihanna, open a bottle of bubbly or vodka and cranberry juice, and that's where the night begins. It should be a real treat to dress up and get yourself looking fabulous; it shouldn't be a chore. It makes me feel really good about myself, and particularly now that I am talking to other boys and back on that scene, it gives me the confidence I need. It's quite scary starting all over again, but if I think I look good, then I can do anything. Here are a few of my going-out tips.

Going-out Tips – Be Prepared

If you know you're going out, get prepared and organised, especially if it's a date. Leave at least three hours to get yourself looking your best. I've made no secret of the fact that I am a big fan of fake tan and I think it gives you a really healthy glow. In particular, if you use it on your face properly, your make-up will sit really well over it.

Applying your make-up well makes a big difference to how you look by the end of the night, and if you do it well, you should only have to re-touch rather than reapply the whole lot every couple of hours.

So, you have your base of fake tan and you've moisturised. Now it's time to apply your make-up. First, put on foundation with a brush or sponge and be careful to apply it to your neck as well so that you don't get a nasty tide mark along the jawline. Contouring is a fantastic way of showing off your features and making your cheekbones as angular as you can without seeing a surgeon! Once your foundation is on, then apply a make-up must – bronzer. Always put bronzer on your cheekbones and forehead, leaving the middle of the face paler. This gives your face a really good shape and defines your cheekbones.

I'm really into my brows and think it's important to give them a good shape. I have mine threaded. I always use highlighter under them to open up my eyes. I use a shimmery Mac highlighter, but you can use any one as long as it's a silver or gold and has a bit of a sparkle to it. Apply it under the brow and over the eye socket – it also makes a good base for your eye shadow.

I use a small, very soft brush to put on eye shadow. I put a lighter colour in the middle of the eye towards the socket to open up the eye and then go darker towards the outer part of the lid. If you fancy the glam look, apply fake lashes. There are amazingly realistic ones or you can go proper fake and get an all-singing, all-dancing jazzy pair. I've worn ones made from feathers and ones with sparkly bits on them – they are great fun and fashionable.

Next up and very important is eyeliner. Steady your

hand and, using a very fine brush (Mac do a great one), run the brush along the top of your eye. Never use it on the bottom of your eye, because if you do, it makes your eyes look smaller. You want to open your eyes and make them look as big as possible. Another trick is to just use mascara on the bottom lashes or to apply a faint line of eye shadow under the bottom lashes to accentuate your eyes.

Last up is your lips. Don't fall into the trap of a) not using lip liner because it's something your mum used in the 1980s or b) using it as it's supposed to be used as a lip liner. I'll let you into a secret – you need to cover the *whole lip* with lip liner, not just the outline, and put lip balm over the top. This gives the illusion of much fuller lips. I use 'Spice' by Mac. Sometimes I like using lipsticks, but I only really like nude colours because they make your lips look fuller.

It's all about making the best of what you have got. There are parts of my body that I hate, like my legs and arms, so if you're wearing a short-sleeved top or a short skirt, then rub in Face and Body by Mac all over the skin to smooth it. It has a really slimming effect. #bonus

Having my hair done is really important to me. I never go out without having it blow-dried and styled before. I have had hair extensions in now for about a year and I love them. There are loads of different kinds of extensions you can have, but I have Tatiana extensions and I get them done in their London branch every three or four months. They make my hair feel so thick, and I love that when I style my hair, it always holds.

I get a lot of compliments about my hair. People ask me all the time how I get my hair to stay so full-looking after a night out and how I manage to keep the curl of a blow-dry in. The secret is honestly my hair extensions. That's not me trying to get a freebie. That is genuinely the reason my hair holds so well. I have quite thick hair naturally, but the extensions are amazing for styling and body. Some extensions need a fair bit of upkeep (you sometimes have to be careful what shampoos you use when you wash your hair, but the better the extension, the less high maintenance they are), but mine are hassle-free – I don't have to worry what shampoos or conditioners I use, and when I get up in the morning, my hair still looks more or less as though it's just been blow-dried. The thickness and movement in 'real' hair extensions mean that you get a lot more body when you put your hair up, and when it's down, it never looks a mess.

I just wanna say that the hair extensions I have are ethical. I know a lot of people don't know where the hair originates from, but I checked all that out before

I went ahead with it. The hair Tatiana uses is really good-quality Russian and European virgin hair. All the hair is hand-arranged so that the cuticles face the same direction from root to end and then your hair doesn't get all tangled up. Virgin hair means that it hasn't been permed, tinted or coloured, and because of that, it is just like your own hair and blends in really naturally. The extensions are quite expensive – they cost me anywhere between £600 and £1,000 each time I get them done – but they are addictive and I can't see myself ever taking them out! I've got an addictive personality – just look at the fake-tan issue I had – and hair extensions are my most recent addiction.

Having extensions must be bad for your natural hair if you keep them in for years and years because they pull at the root and your own hair gets weaker, but I love them too much to part with. A lot of my friends have them in and have bald spots when you look closely, but once you've worn them, it's hard to let them go. I feel bare without them and as though I have hardly any hair.

My friend Katie Price has them in and she's the same as me – she can't bear to part with them. She has had hers for something like twelve years, so that'll probably be me in twelve years' time too! Actually, I'll be eighty years old with them still in! I'm serious – I know I should give my hair a break, but I don't want to. I think I'm gonna have to live with the bald spots if that happens. They take a while to put in each time, about three to four hours, which is tedious, but these days my life is so crazy and hectic that it's about the only time I have to catch up with emails and texts. I rarely wash my own hair now. Most of the time I pop into my salon and get it done – it's only down the road. That sounds lazy, doesn't it? But it's just my life is so manic that it gives me a few moments to sit still! Having said that, it's fairly crazy at my salon too, with lots of fans coming in, and it's important for me to spend some time with them and have pictures taken and give autographs and all that. I'm here because of them and I won't forget that.

I have my hair washed and blow-dried every three days depending on photo shoots and events, but that's how often it needs doing. If I can't get there for some reason, I sometimes use dry shampoo to freshen it up – like when I was practising on the rink for *Dancing on Ice*, which training started for just after I left *TOWIE* last August. I spent so much time rehearsing and trying to make sure I didn't make a fool out of myself that I often didn't get a chance to go to the salon. Luckily, dry shampoo does the trick quickly and effectively. It's also really good if you don't have extensions in. I used to use it a lot when I was styling my hair and it seemed to hold the style better and for longer.

Having your hair done is really important to complete a look for going out – it doesn't feel right going out with your face all nicely made up and your hair an afterthought. It adds the finishing touch, I think, and for me is probably the most important ingredient to looking good. I need my hair to feel and look nice or I can't go out.

Once my hair and make-up are done, it's all about the outfit. I never get dressed until I am completely ready. I wear a whitish towelling dressing gown while I'm getting ready. I say 'whitish' because it is covered in make-up and fake tan! Fashion is my passion and I love choosing outfits and teaming them with great shoes and handbags.

It sounds weird even saying this, but I now have a stylist called Donna Louise who helps me. Like I said, these days it's not so easy just to pop to Lakeside for the day with my mates. My work schedule is manic and I barely have a moment to myself, let alone time to go into town and browse the shops. Donna always wanted to be a stylist and she emailed my agent to see if she could help me out, so I thought I'd take her up on the offer. She has never done styling one on one before and is kind of learning on the job. She's been helping me for about six months now and has become a really good friend. I don't know what I'd do without her – she organises all my outfits for different dos and collects them for me when I haven't got time. She is brilliant. Oh my God, it sounds really lovey that I have a stylist, doesn't it? It's not like that, though – she just helps me out so that I'm not panicking about what I'm wearing or how I am going to look. If I've got an event to go to, I need to look good to feel confident.

She will advise me and suggest things that will suit and make the best of my figure. I choose and then she sorts the outfit out for me. It's pretty amazing because with her contacts she speaks to the shops and organises times for me to go in and have a look at their new collections before they hit the shelves. I'm like a kid in a sweetshop. It's amazing but weird. I sometimes think, How can this be happening to me? I have to pinch myself to know that it's all real.

When Donna first started working with me, it was a bit weird and I wasn't sure it was going to work, because I know what I like and what I want to wear, and Donna wanted to dress me in a certain way. I am pretty headstrong with things like fashion and I like what I like. I don't feel happy wearing something completely out of my comfort zone and I think she gets that now, though at the beginning we clashed on some things.

Fashion changes all the time, and if you look at what I'm wearing this year in comparison to what I was wearing last year, there is a massive difference. I was plainer then, whereas now I am single and going out more and I'm happier to try out new things. I'm trying cooler, more on-trend fashions and I'm really enjoying experimenting. I think age helps. I was twenty-six last September, and as I am getting older, I have more confidence to try new things and not worry so much about other people as long as I feel good. Fashion is so personal that you shouldn't judge others' ideas. Take vajazzling – it doesn't float my boat at all. What's the point of it? I would kind of get it if you had it on your arm or shoulder, but on your fanny?! I have never been interested in it, but each to their own, and I know lots of girls round here love it. To me, it's weird.

Although Donna now works with me, I still love shopping in my favourite high-street shops like Zara, Topshop, Miss Selfridge and River Island when I get the chance. I am very fortunate because I get sent a lot of things from different fashion houses, such as Celeb Boutique and Forever Unique, so I get to wear amazing fashion without even having to leave the house to shop for it. How cool is that? I get pictured a lot, and I try to wear clothes that are unique and a bit different, and Donna is great at finding those kinds of outfits for me.

I like designer things, but it's not something I'm hung up on. I would prefer to spend my money on a classic handbag or pair of shoes than an outfit that I might only wear once. You can be wearing a high-street dress and team it with a good bag and shoes and it will set off the whole outfit. No one will know or care that the outfit cost £30. Look at what I wore to the *Magic Mike* première in London last July – it's a really good example of how you can wear an affordable dress and set it off with designer shoes and a designer handbag. I was wearing a Hybrid yellow dress, which wasn't very expensive, about £80 and I teamed it with a Vivienne Westwood patent clutch and Lady Daf patent Christian Louboutins.

I have a few decent handbags and shoes, like Chanel, Vivienne Westwood, Mulberry and Hermès. I have bought them all for myself. I have saved up for them, and then when it's been my birthday or a special occasion, I have treated myself. I love Louboutins and I really wanted a pair of Lady Peep Spikes in red. Oh my God, I was desperate for a pair. It had been a really busy week with work and I thought, Sod it. I deserve it. I work really hard and I'm going to treat myself. So I did. And I love them! But my pocket is

£900 lighter. It's weird to think I can spend that sort of money on a pair of shoes when just a few years ago, I was a receptionist earning hardly any money.

There was only one other time that I did something that rash and I bought a Chanel bag. It cost me £3,000. I know that's a heap of money, but it was a dream I'd had since I was a kid to own a Chanel handbag and I did it all by myself. Shoes and handbags are definitely my thing. I sound extravagant, but I only have a few and they are classics. Even with jewellery I don't have much, just dress jewellery, and I only wear it if I think it complements what I'm wearing. Most of the time I prefer not to wear any, because I think it detracts from the outfit.

My Going-out iPod Playlist

Usher – 'Appetite' and 'Let Me See'

Rihanna – 'Diamonds' ♥

Mariah Carey – 'Migrate'

Drake – 'Successful'

Kirko Bangz – 'Drank in My Cup'

Beyoncé (OMG, I love her) – 'Diva', 'Upgrade U'
and 'Halo'

J Lo – 'I'm Into You' and 'Love Don't Cost a Thing'

Dressing for Your Shape

I have a curvy body. It's toned, but it's curvy. I have boobs and a bum, which means that I'm not straight up and down, so I have to choose my clothes carefully. I think some people think that if you have a curvy frame, you have to cover it up in baggy clothes, but I totally disagree. I wear fitted clothes, but clothes that fit in the right places. I know what won't suit my figure, so there's no point in trying to cram it into something meant for a skinny bean. I have been there and done that and it looks unflattering and makes me look bigger than I really am.

Focus on the smallest part of your body and make the most of it – you want to draw attention to that part of you rather than the bits you don't like so much! I'm conscious about my arms and legs, so to accentuate my figure, I'll often wear a high-waisted knee-length skirt. The eye is instantly drawn to the top of the skirt, which is most people's thinnest area, but it's also important that the bottom of the skirt is tight round the knee so you can see a shape. A full skirt would make you look bigger than you are. I also like to wear peplum dresses – they are really flattering to my figure, as well as being chic and trendy. You can buy them fairly reasonably and dress them up or down according to the event. Peplum dresses are also great for people who have figures that are straight up and down and have very little shape, because they automatically give the illusion that they have curves.

Baggy and flowing is best really for tall and skinny people with good legs because they look willowy. If I wear a baggy dress, I need to wear a high-waisted belt with a buckle to draw the eye to my smallest part. If I don't, the dress will look like a sack on me and will make me look big.

Shoes really set off an outfit, but I hate shoes with straps round the ankle – they cut off your legs and make you look short and stumpy. I always want to elongate my legs by wearing high-heel peep toes or pointy shoes, which also slim your legs. I find high platform shoes are very slimming too – they make you taller and make you stand properly. Kitten heels wouldn't do anything for me, as they make my legs look awful.

It's really important for everyone to dress according to their shape. None of us is the same, so if a certain look doesn't suit you, try and come up with your own variation that is cool and on trend, but makes the best of what you've got. It's also important to take into account things like skin tone and hair colour, which play a massive part in what you look good in and what suits you. For example, some people don't suit yellows or oranges. Pale people can often look drained if they wear those lighter colours, and if they wear black, they can look quite gothy.

Last year at the National Television Awards, I wore a J Lo dress. I bought it in the States and really liked it, but when I went to put it on that night, it didn't look right. I got ready in a rush, which I hate doing – it makes me edgy anyway – and I had no time to change. The press completely laid into me. The thing is, the dress was OK and it cost me a lot of money, but that night it didn't look right. It was matt, but in all the pictures it looked shiny. It was such a waste of a good dress and I was battered for it. When I look back, I think it may well have been because my hair was so dark. Now my hair is lighter, maybe it would be OK. Both hair colour and skin tone can be the difference between a style hit and a miss.

I, more than anyone, know what it's like to live with a curvy frame, and now I live with one under the media spotlight. My body seems to have become a regular talking point for magazines and newspapers, and I do get a lot of flak, and you know what? I think the more they have a go at me, the more I put on weight. As much as I say I don't care, there is a part of me that does. I wouldn't be normal if I didn't get a bit upset by some of the articles written about me and the online comments people leave branding me 'fat'. I'm always criticised for wearing 'unflattering' outfits, but I wear clothes that I think suit my figure and that I feel happy in. I might get it wrong occasionally, but who doesn't? I know what I like to wear and what makes me feel good and that's not gonna change, no matter how much they lay into me. A few months ago I wouldn't have said that, but as the days and weeks go by, I feel like I'm getting more and more confident.

At the end of last year some of the press were really harsh about me and I'd be lying if I said that didn't get to me – it did. Although the articles slating my appearance do knock me now and again, these days, even when I am feeling horribly low, I refuse to let the bastards get to me. I tell myself, If I feel good, then that's what's important.

Enhancing Curves

Curves are something to be proud of and shouldn't be hidden away – make the most of them!

I've talked about high-waisted belts a lot, but I'm a big fan of them. They are really good at drawing your eye to your smallest part, round your ribcage and under your boobs. It's a nice touch to have a buckle or something on the belt too as a focal point and can make the belt even more slimming. I love leather. Lol. I'm really into leather at the moment and I've got a pair of Kim Kardashian leather trousers and a pair from Zara, but they need to be fitted in the right places or they have a potential to make you look big. My Kim Kardashian trousers are tight in the leg but quite baggy round the bum and aren't that flattering, but my Zara ones I love.

Skinny jeans are very fashionable, but if you have bigger legs like me, then buy skinnies with elastic in them – Miss Selfridge do some really good ones. I have them in black and blue. I think high-waisted flares are probably the most flattering jeans. I wore a pair when I first went to meet my agent, Max Clifford, for lunch before he took me on. I was papped that day and can remember seeing the pictures and being happy with the way I looked. They elongate your legs, particularly if you team them with a high heel.

One of the looks I hate is girls with those awful stuck-on boob jobs. If you have a boob job, then cover up rather than showing them off – it looks really cheap and tacky. Sexy is great, but the more boobs are pushed up, particularly if they are fake, the more slutty the look. If I had my boobs done, I'd want to make them appear as natural as possible. Big boobs can also make you look top-heavy. They enhance your waist because they are so big, but they can often make you look broad and bigger than you are. Katie Price has fake boobs and in pictures she can quite often look bigger than she really is, because in the flesh she is tiny.

How to Accessorise

As I said earlier, I hate too much jewellery and rarely wear any. I would never wear a watch and a bracelet and a ring and earrings. It's too much and it cheapens everything. It's like overkill. Never wear a necklace and earrings – one or the other. If you've got a nice watch, wear that, but not a bracelet as well. Make a statement with what you wear rather than stuffing it all on. You don't know where to look if you do!

What to Wear on a Date

Most importantly, be classy not slutty. On a first date you want to give the impression of the girl next door, and if you get too dressed up, you'll have nothing to wear on the next date when you go to a club. Lol. A nice pair of jeans and a shirt with a big bag looks really simple but effective. Or a knee-length dress and a jacket. *Never* go over the top. I think boys prefer girls who look as though they are effortless. They like the more natural look. However long it takes to get, remember that first and all-important impression. There's plenty of time to show them that you can get properly done up on another date. If you do it on the first date, I think it comes across as desperate and makes you feel uncomfortable.

Interview Outfits

Always be smart, like in a peplum dress or a fitted jacket and trousers. The look shouldn't be over the top and 'try hard'. Definitely *no* jewellery – it gives off a tacky look. If you really feel you have to wear something, then go for a nice watch, but nothing else. Hair should be in an up-do or smooth and straight and curled under. Wear minimal make-up so you look smart and clean.

Beachwear

When I went to Miami last year on holiday, I nearly cancelled because I was so unhappy with where my body was at and when I did decide to go, I got papped and they are some of the worst pictures I have ever seen of myself. The body fascists were quick to get online and make horrible comments, which made me even more conscious of how I looked. I would cover up all the time with a kaftan or a sarong – anything that would conceal my legs and tummy. You can buy matching bikini sets and sarongs if you're feeling body-conscious like me, but there are a few tips I have to make the best of your body on the beach.

Firstly, I think pant bikinis are way more flattering than the ones that do up with string round the side. The string can cut into your skin and make it look flabby, and you can get a muffin-top. I've also learned that with swimwear you should buy a size up from your usual clothing size. Don't worry that it's a size up – no one is ever gonna ask you what size bikini you are in

– but it'll instantly be more flattering to your body. Cut the labels out if it bothers you that much.

Wedding Outfits

Always wear something beautiful and elegant. Be plain but classy and opt for an outfit that looks expensive. Put your hair in an up-do and finish the look with small diamond earrings. I would never wear black or white to a wedding, and definitely nothing too short.

Clubbing Outfits

It really depends on how you are feeling, but Hybrid dresses always look good and are really comfortable. I never seem to get bad comments if I wear one.

I'm not a fan of lots of glitz, as too much can look really over the top. When I went to the BAFTAs in 2011, I wore a Giovanni dress, which I got in the sale. It was proper sparkly, but I'm not sure I should have had my hair up. The dress was so over the top that I think my hair needed to be more simple. If I wore it again, I'd wear my hair down and wavy. All of us looked over the top. There's a picture of me, Amy Childs, Lydia Bright and Sam Faiers and it's funny because we all look a bit glitzy and overly made up. Amy looks as though she is sat on a toilet-roll holder!

If I'm wearing something short to go clubbing, I like to wear a long-sleeve or three-quarter-length-sleeve top to go with it. Because I don't like my legs or my arms, if one is on show, the other needs to be covered up! I'm not a fan of wearing a short skirt and a low-cut top. It needs to be one or the other. Having both exposed can make you look cheap. I like shoulder pads, though – they are a good trick to make you look slimmer round the waist. Go on, give them a go!

How to Pose for a Picture

It's all in the pose, believe me. Don't ever look straight into the camera – I think that's the most unflattering pose. Instead turn your head slightly sideways, but keep your eyes focused on the lens. Drop your head down, but keep your eyes fixed on that lens. Finally, pout to make your lips look full.

For full-length snaps, do the same, but turn sideways, bending your leg and your arm closest to the camera.

I don't always remember my own advice, though. Sometimes when I get caught unawares by a pap, I know the next day there will be a load of pictures splashed everywhere that I hate.

PS Looking good is not just a girl thing; men need to take care of themselves too. I like a man who is clean and tidy but balanced – with him not spending more time in the bathroom than me. (That would be wrong.) Some girls like tattoos on a bloke, but I've never really been into them unless they are classy and not in your face. I prefer smart boys. There's nothing better than a man in a suit that fits. Too many blokes wear clothes that don't fit them properly, and you can generally tell what they're like by their suit. If he takes care of himself, then his suit will be fitted in all the right places. A guy who turns up looking unpolished isn't for me.

To be honest, I'm just beginning to learn what I do and don't like after so many years with Mark. I became kind of institutionalised because I knew nothing else but how he was. It was a bit scary starting again, but I'm enjoying it now and am having fun being on the dating scene. It's a new chapter and for once I am enjoying the attention and I'm not gonna feel guilty about it.

3

Finding Love, Losing Love and
Looking for Love

I HATE THAT people think I'm some kind of desperate ex. How embarrassing. If only people knew the truth about my relationship with Mark Wright, I think I'd be judged a bit less harshly. I've never wanted to 'tell all' and I don't intend doing it now, because Mark will always be a big part of my life and my past. We were together for eleven years, he knows everything about me, and he has shaped who I am today. He was the love of my life. Having said that, things have got to that point where I have to tell my side of the story, from the beginning: the good times, the bad times, everything. I've had enough of seeing lies printed about me. Lately it feels as if Mark is ignoring me and can barely bring himself to acknowledge that we even had a relationship. It does hurt because he is the one person who knows me better than anyone and who can hurt me the most. I feel as though he must hate me and does things just to wind me up. I'm not gonna rise to it and play stupid games, though. Instead I'm going to try and explain things from my perspective and put the record straight. It's about time everybody knew the truth.

Mark and I went to school together, but we didn't start dating until we were fifteen years old. Mark only lived a couple of roads down from me, but I never clocked him until we were put in a maths class together. He kept looking at me and I would smile back. It was obvious that we fancied each other. Lol. Mark had been with a few girls and was quite popular, so I wasn't too sure about him. He was a good-looking boy, but I wasn't that bothered at the beginning – it was more the other way round. He was quite romantic, though. He asked one of my friends for my number because he was too shy to ask me for it and he rang me that night while I was in the bath. He said to me afterwards that I was offish with him, which I don't think he'd been used to! We arranged to meet up the following evening, so after school he came and knocked for me at my mum's house. We went on the longest walk from my house in Loughton where we moved to from Chigwell to his house in Buckhurst Hill through the forest. It was a summer night, so it was very light and warm, and we really got to know each other. We chatted and chatted and got on so well. I was smitten immediately and can remember going home to my mum afterwards and saying, 'Mum, I think I'm in love.' Being with Mark gave me butterflies, and they never went away.

Our next date was at his house. His family had just moved into a new place and it was completely upside down, with everything everywhere. When I got there, his mum and dad were out and we lay on the sofa together. It was all very innocent. I would never put out on the first few dates. If that's what you want to do, fine – have some fun – but if you want a relationship and you want the boy to respect you, then sleeping with him too soon will give the impression you are a bit cheap. I was all giggly and silly – I was already head over heels in love – and when he kissed me that first time, it was the best kiss ever. I could feel he really liked me and he was full of compliments, saying I was beautiful and that he had met 'the one'. He was a proper charmer and I was putty in his hands.

I was so embarrassed when his parents came home that night and we were lying on the sofa together. I kind of jumped up like a naughty kid! That was the first time I'd met them, and I also met his little sister, Natalya, who was only a year and a half. She was so cute. I loved her. His parents ordered Chinese for us all and for once I felt part of a family. I was so happy.

As time went on, we spent more and more time together. It became massively intense between us very quickly and within a month we were with each other every day of the week. He would stay at mine more often than not. Carol, Mark's mum, didn't like us staying in the same room together at her house; I'd be made to sleep in another room. Now I'm older, I can understand why she wasn't happy, but when everyone was asleep, I'd creep into his room! #sneaky

After a while Mark more or less moved into my mum's house, because she was cool about us being together and she really liked him. Mark and Mum always got on well; in fact if we ever had a row, she would often take his side, which would really piss me off. We would bunk off school together a lot and sneak back to the house. It felt naughty and passionate and exciting. He used to say that this could be the start of a marriage and I had flutters in the pit of my stomach. We couldn't get enough of one another – we were each other's obsession.

If we couldn't be together, we would continually

text each other saying we loved and missed each other, and when we were at school, in class, we would spend half the lesson writing letters to one another and passing them across the room, trying not to be caught by the teachers. It was crazy love, but it was so much fun. When we did our GCSEs, we managed to sit next to each other in the exam hall and we made sure we had the same answers. Lol. We both did OK and passed, but my grades were really average. I think I was so in love I couldn't be bothered to revise. We did that in all tests and exams – we would cheat and help each other out. We were inseparable and in our own little bubble. We dropped everything, including our friends, so that we spent virtually every waking moment together. When we stayed at each other's houses, we'd spend the whole night kissing and cuddling and playing silly games. When we watched a film, we'd always miss half of it because we were so into each other. We were joined at the hip!

We were only sixteen, but it was all about the two of us, even at that early stage. Mark wanted us to go away together. I just wanted to be with him and couldn't wait to go away just the two of us.

I had my nails done and a wax the day before we went. I remember I was so excited about our first holiday together, I was like a silly, giggly kid. We stayed at his uncle's place near Alicante and it was one of the best holidays we had together. His parents came too, but they stayed in a hotel down the road, which meant we could have private time together. Our relationship had been stormy from the start, but that holiday there was only one row – over me having a glass of wine that his cousin bought for me – and when we were rowing I got knocked into the Jacuzzi, fully clothed! Afterwards we made up and went back to our room, put on a movie and fell asleep. Rows and making up were normal for us.

I remember we barely left the house that holiday, and it was then that I knew I wanted to spend the rest of my life with this boy. We were so alike: we laughed at the same things; we loved the same food; we wanted the same things for our future, like marriage and kids. It seemed so perfect, and even though it was all-consuming, we both felt the same way. We spoke about our future all the time and I couldn't wait to get older so I could marry him and be the mother of his children. In a way I thought that I could finally have the family that I never had and had always wanted. It all sounds immature and stupid now, but I really thought that we had a connection and I believed in us.

I knew I could be the wife he wanted, because he used to tell me how much he loved the way I was homely and he found it attractive in me that I loved children. We talked a lot about having our own family and we chose names for our kids. Mark wanted boys, so of course one was going to be Mark (original!), one Charlie after his granddad and Eddie because he liked it! I would have preferred more unusual names, but that's what he wanted and I was content to go along with that. I knew I could be what he wanted me to be, and I knew I could make him happy. We talked about all sorts of things. It was so intense between us that we even agreed that if we died and we were married, then we would be put in the same coffin. We'd have random conversations like that all the time.

We also had a great physical relationship, and he frequently told me that I was the best girl he had ever been with and that he loved my body. He loved my boobs especially because they were big, but not too big, and they were real.

Our next holiday to Egypt was even better. We didn't leave the resort once and we had a brilliant time sunbathing and chilling out. I think that was the only holiday when we didn't have a row – probably because it was just us. If there was an outside influence, it would always cause trouble between us.

Looking back, Mark was always questioning me from day one, but at first I acted like I didn't care, and that seemed to really bother him. I remember one time he went mad because a boy gave me a lift to a party. He was just a friend from school, and it was a nice gesture – nothing more. Besides, I was with two other girls. We arrived at the party and I met up with Mark. I didn't tell him how I'd got there – because there wasn't anything to tell – and we had a really nice night together. The next day, though, Mark called me out of a lesson at school. He made me go just outside the school grounds, where no one could overhear us, and he went mental. I couldn't understand why. He was so angry with me. He said, 'You are never to get in another boy's car. Never.' I realised that someone had told him about the lift to the party the night before. He was going ballistic, even though *nothing* had happened, and he was totally unreasonable. I was like, 'Mark, just listen to me. You're getting the hump over nothing. Nothing happened. It was just a lift, and I was with two other mates.' He wasn't listening to what I was saying. He just seemed mad with me and that was that. I knew in that moment that he had real issues with other people, but in a weird way I liked it – I thought that if he was jealous, then he must care about me, and he didn't want any other girl. I guess that was the control Mark had over me, and as time went on, it got more extreme.

When we left school, Mark won a scholarship to play football for Tottenham Hotspur, and I got my first job, in Level One, a hairdresser's in Buckhurst Hill. Mark would come to the salon most days and wait until I finished so that we could walk home together. We'd have dinner at his mum's house and then go back to mine to stay the night. It was at this point, after we'd left school, that the cracks in our relationship really started to show. Our relationship became increasingly stormy.

I wasn't a jealous person by nature at all, but as the relationship progressed, I somehow got more and more insecure too. I think jealousy breeds jealousy. Mark questioned my every move, so I started to question his as well. We were very young when we got together, so all of Mark's mates were single and they wanted him to be single too so that they could go on the pull. That made me even more panicky while I was sat at home night after night waiting for him. It's funny because at the beginning he was probably more bothered about me than I was about him, but the more time went on, the more I began to feel as though I should be grateful for being with him, and that's when I started to get insecure too. I don't think anyone thinks of Mark as the jealous or insecure person in our relationship – it's me who has been labelled as the obsessive one and the one who can't let go. That pisses me off a lot because it's simply not like that.

Things started to take a real turn for the worse when we got to an age where we both wanted to be going out clubbing and to bars. Mark seemed to hate me going out with him. I know that sounds weird to most people, but it became normal to me. He made me feel like it was OK for couples not to go out together, that it was right, even though deep down I knew that it was wrong. If I did ever go out with him, which was very rare, he made me feel that I was cramping his style. He would quite often behave really differently when we were out with people to how he did when we were at our parents' alone together. I found his behaviour quite confusing and at times upsetting. I'd say to him, 'Why don't you want me out with you? Why can't we go out like a normal couple?' He'd say to me, 'Lauren, I don't like it when you are drunk.' I think it was just an excuse, though, because I'm not a nasty drunk at all. A lot of our rows would be over drink and because he wouldn't let me have any. He never saw what I was like drunk and that I'm not an ugly one. I'd sometimes snap and say to him, 'Why can't I have a drink? Why is it OK for you and not for me?' but mostly I just tried to keep the peace.

Looking back I suspect that what it boiled down to was jealousy, his wandering eye and making sure I was at home waiting for him when he wanted me. I allowed everything to be on his terms. I can't believe that this felt normal at the time. If we did ever go out, we'd never have a relaxed evening. Most of the time I felt on edge because I didn't know how he would be. I like a drink, but because Mark hated me drinking, he'd suddenly snap, say I couldn't have any more and just take my glass off me. He, of course, was allowed to drink. I didn't mind him drinking because he was always very sweet when he'd had a drink – he was lovey and kissy and cuddly.

Pretty soon Mark made it clear that not only did he not want me to go out to pubs with him, but it felt like he didn't want me going out at all. At the beginning I was still quite strong and would go anyway, but I'd have a crap time because in the back of my mind I thought Mark would be angry with me when I got home. I wouldn't let him know that I had a rubbish time. I'd pretend like I was having the best time, which wound him up.

Little by little I was giving him more and more control over my life. One of my really good friends, Charlotte Lubin, used to try and make me see sense occasionally. She didn't get why I was so worried about what Mark thought about this or that, or why I let him have a say in the things I did. She always used to say to me, 'How do you do it, Lauren? It's not normal!' She didn't get it at all! My other friends didn't often say much about it. Occasionally they were like, 'Lauren, why do you put up with that crap?' But I did, and they knew that I was willing to put up with a lot – more than most probably.

Mark would comment on the way I looked as well as where I went. He didn't like me wearing low-cut tops or short skirts. Once, he saw a short skirt that I'd bought and refused to let me wear it. He said he hated everything fake, even fake tan, and he hated me wearing the stuff. He hated it, but I loved it and didn't wanna look pale.

One day, even though he hated the stuff, I talked him into letting me put some fake tan on his face. The thing is, I forgot to do his neck, so the next day, when he went to football training, he had a brown face and white neck. I think he saw the funny side, but he was ridiculed by the rest of the team! That's the thing about Mark – he can get so annoyed about something and then other times find things funny and a bit of a joke. Underneath it all, even when he was angry, I knew he loved me and somehow that made up for the bad times.

I have always been a party girl and love going to a club to dance, but Mark had major issues with me going out because he didn't trust me. I found it hard because I loved to have fun and knew I would never be unfaithful to him, but I couldn't make him understand that. I was so blinded by the love that I had for him that I didn't really kick up about it. If it was what Mark wanted I was happy to go along with it. Now I look back and realise I didn't stand up for myself enough, but back then I didn't know any different. I would sit up and wait for him when he went out – sometimes half the night. I'd hate it, thinking about what he could be getting up to without me. Instead of feeling happy, I'd feel lonely. I felt like I did when I was a child.

On Friday nights he wouldn't be able to go out because he had football training the next morning, so I'd spend the evening with him, instead of being out with my friends. I missed friends' birthday parties and going out with my mates. I lost nearly all my childhood friends because I was so wrapped up in being with Mark. I suppose it was no surprise that in the end all

I really had around me were Mark and his family. I
became kind of isolated. That's one thing I have learned,
big time: I will never chuck friends for a relationship
ever again. I had to learn that the hard way, but after
a slightly dysfunctional childhood, I massively craved
love and did more or less as I was told. The sad truth
is that I would rather have been with Mark than with
my mates. I was infatuated with him and I wanted to
make him happy. Sometimes I resented missing nights
out but if that was going to make Mark unhappy, I
didn't want to see that.

I really don't want to paint a bad picture of Mark,
because I did love him. Why else would I have stayed
with him? He made me feel safe and secure, and at the
beginning, that was what I'd needed and been looking
for. It was only over time that things became unhealthy,
and by that point of course I was in too deep. I
convinced myself that the way we were living as a couple
was normal.

I think Christmases with Mark were my favourite
times with him. They became really special for us.
Every Christmas Eve he would call my mum and
organise to drop my presents round at the house. He
would tell her, 'Do *not* let Lauren open them before
tomorrow, OK?' We rarely spent the night together on
Christmas Eve, and although I missed him, it was kind

of exciting too because I knew he was coming round with my presents and it made me feel special that he'd thought so carefully about what to get me. I desperately wanted to open the presents, but, like I say, Mum was under strict instructions not to let me. I used to have butterflies all night. Mark and I might have been together for eleven years, but neither of us ever lost that feeling. I miss that. ☹ Mark would spoil me rotten and buy me the best Christmas presents. He would only really buy for me and no one else. Out of all my presents I'd look forward to getting his the most. Lol. In fact, I only really cared about his presents – they were amazing. He wasn't big on buying me anything in between birthdays and Christmases, but on those occasions I was spoiled. I'd wake up on Christmas Day really excited and go straight to them. I couldn't get them open quickly enough! Ripping off all the wrapping paper and opening the boxes, I was like a small child!

One year I can remember there was a small box under the tree. When I tore off the paper and opened it, I wanted to cry, I was so happy. He had bought me a pair of Chanel earrings. They were the best present that I'd ever received and I was on cloud nine! I couldn't believe that I actually owned a pair! He could be so thoughtful. If I'd seen something when I was out shopping that I'd liked, he'd remember and go back and get it for me. He was romantic like that and caring.

Even the Christmas before last (2011), when we weren't officially seeing each other, we spent time together. We went to Faces in Gants Hill and he had a few. He was all over me and I liked it because he wasn't very often like that in public.

Aside from those special occasions like Christmas and my birthday, things with Mark were by this point becoming increasingly stormy. My rebellious streak started coming out. Mark used to go out every Saturday night with his mates and I stopped telling him what my plans were. I would get all dressed up to go out and then put my dressing gown on over the top and wear my slippers, so that when Mark came round before his night out, he would think I was going to bed. I'd tell him I was tired and was off to bed. Then the minute he was gone, the dressing gown would come off and I'd go out for the evening! Unsurprisingly, it massively backfired in the end, because one time Mark called the house phone, probably to check up on me, and Mum didn't lie for me, which really pissed me off. When I got back that evening, he was there waiting in my bed and he wasn't very happy. He looked at me and quite calmly said,

'Where have you been, Lauren? I thought you were staying in.' It was horrible because I knew he was furious and seeing him lying there having basically caught me out was the worst feeling. I was like, 'I just popped out with my friends. I didn't mean to upset you or hurt you. You know that I love you.' I tried everything to smooth things over because I was frightened he was about to end it. He had threatened in the past that he would dump me if I secretly went out with my mates, and that night I really thought he might, but he didn't of course.

My rebellious streak continued for a time. One particular night will stay with me for ever. Again it happened after another of those times when I'd gone out despite Mark telling me not to. Looking back, I think he thought he'd teach me a lesson. I think we were about seventeen at the time. I'd been out and had stayed over at my friend's house. At 6 a.m. my mobile rang. The number that flashed up on screen was my home number, so I quickly answered it. It was Mark and he said he was at my house waiting for me, so I jumped into a cab and rushed back to him, wondering what the hell he was gonna be like. I thought he would be annoyed, but he wasn't. Instead he was all over me, being affectionate and kissing and cuddling me. I felt something was up straight away.

We were lying in bed together and I asked him over and over what he had been doing that evening, until he eventually told me that he'd been to a hotel with a group of friends, including some girls. I wondered what they had got up to. My body felt numb, and my chest felt tight. I pleaded, 'Don't tell me. I don't want to know.' Somehow I felt that if he didn't tell me, then nothing could have happened. I wanted to bury my head in the sand. He told me again and again nothing had happened and how much he loved me and that I was the only girl for him. I wanted to believe him so much, and I didn't want us to break up.

Silently, I cried all night, so as not to wake him. Eventually I stayed in all weekend while he went out, and it put a lot of pressure on us. For anyone, I think a situation like that would be suffocating. It had got to that stage where going out was too much of a headache. I made the decision that all I wanted was to be with Mark, and if me being at home made him happy, then that's what I'd do. Each week I would hope that he wouldn't make plans for the Saturday night and that we could have the evening together. If we did, I'd always book Cafe Spice on Loughton High Road. I loved those evenings. I'd spend my usual time getting ready, doing my hair and make-up, and looking my best, and then we'd walk there hand in hand. We would have a lovely meal and banter like any normal couple. We'd have a proper laugh. We'd only have eyes for each other and wouldn't notice anything else going on in the restaurant. We'd then walk back hand in hand and watch *My Father the Hero*, and then he'd watch *Match of the Day*. They were the best times, and I felt so happy and safe when it was just us.

On his eighteenth birthday he wanted to go out on his own. No change there. He got a limo with his mates and went to Embassy. I stayed at his house and waited for him to come home, but he didn't. All night I sat there and waited and waited. I tried to call him, but his phone was off. I texted him, but nothing. He eventually rolled in at 6 a.m. still wearing his suit. Although I was relieved to see him, I felt uneasy. He couldn't understand why I was upset.

The next day I went on the club's website, which Mark and I always had a look at, and there he was with glamour models draped around him. He passed it off as nothing, as he always did, but it was his eighteenth birthday and he had chosen to celebrate with these girls and not me. It made me feel inadequate and my self-esteem hit an all-time low.

I think deep down I suspected that Mark was up

to no good – why else would he be so adamant that I shouldn't go out with him? – but Mark is a right charmer so he always had a feasible and credible excuse ready for me. I so wanted to believe him, and he made me feel so good when he was with me that I'd go with it. No matter the rows, I'd always stand by him and wait in bed for him to get home. This is gonna sound ridiculous, but I genuinely thought that if I let him get it all out of his system, then when we got married and had children, he would be faithful and a great father. How stupid is that? I really believed that, so every time he did something to make me feel insecure, I would think, It's OK – when we are married, he'll be totally faithful to me. What a f*cking mug.

Even though he kept hurting me and making me feel rubbish, I still loved him so much. When we were on our own together, he made me feel a million dollars and acted like he idolised me. It was the small things that meant the most, like how loving he was to me on Valentine's Day, when he used to send me massive bouquets of flowers or a teddy and heart chocolates, and we'd go to a local restaurant, because Mark isn't a Nobu guy! He used to tell me I was cute. We were like a married couple in a way, but with the romance – we would kiss and cuddle all the time. He used to tell me I'd be a great mum and that no one compared to me.

He had other ways of showing he cared. More recently, for example, when I went on personal appearances (PAs) with Arg, we'd be tired driving home late at night and Mark would ring every two minutes shouting at Argent not to fall asleep behind the wheel. He would really panic that something was going to happen to me. In a funny way it was nice to know that he worried about me.

Things took a dramatic turn for the worse in our relationship when Mark got a job as a club promoter when we were both eighteen. By this point, he had left football and had decided he wanted to make a name for himself. He was out every weekend and he'd invite our mates to his club nights, but I'd just be waiting for him like an idiot. We were quite a fiery couple and sometmes after a big row we would break up, but it would never last long. One day I got a call from a mate saying, 'Have you seen the newspaper?' I was like, 'No. Why?' Mark had been pictured hand in hand leaving Vendome nightclub in Mayfair with a glamour model. I felt sick. I couldn't believe it. Mark told me he was just doing it to get publicity for the club and that she was nothing to him. Mark said we weren't officially together at the time, although I thought we were, so I Facebooked her and asked her what had happened. She basically said that I should ask Mark, but that she hadn't realised he had a girl-friend. I questioned him about it, but still he said it was nothing. I believed him. By this point I was working as a receptionist for Orrick, Herrington & Sutcliffe, an American-owned legal company in the East End, having decided to move on from my job in hairdressing. I loved hairdressing and it gave me something to fall back on but I wanted more for myself. After work, four or five times a week Mark and I would go out for dinner. While I was at work and on those 'going out' days, I would think of nothing else. I'd hide my mobile phone in my bra so that if he called me, I could nip into a meeting room to speak to him, because I wasn't really allowed to at my desk. I longed for the day to end so that I could get home and changed and we could go out. This one night, though, he picked me up in his car, leaned over, took my hands and started to get upset. He told me that whilst we were on a break he had done a magazine shoot with the glamour model saying that they were boyfriend and girlfriend. I was shocked. It didn't sink in. I was thinking, Why? Why would you do this to me? I was really quiet as he told me, but my eyes welled up and that seemed to get to him even more. He said, 'I love you more than anything in the world. You are everything to me. I'm doing this for our future. Please believe me. She means nothing.' I stayed silent. What could I say?

He carried on driving, but when we got to the restaurant, I couldn't eat. He ordered for me, like he always did. I never even used to look at the menu. Some people may think that was odd, but in a way I liked it. I saw it as him taking care of me. That night, though, I couldn't eat a thing and asked him to take me home. I couldn't even look at him.

I can't tell you how it felt when that magazine hit the shelves. All our friends thought of us as a couple and I was a laughing stock round our way. How embarrassing. I was in bits, but I pretended to everyone that I was cool with it, that it meant nothing, so it was OK. When I closed the door behind me that night, though, I cried and cried. Mark phoned me and said he wanted to go through the article with me. I have to say, I was furious and was like, 'Are you f*cking joking?' When he came round, I smacked him over and over in the face. I was going crazy. I still can't believe I did that, and I'm a bit ashamed of it, but he'd pushed me to my limit. My behaviour was completely out of character, and I knew that our relationship was making me go mad. He was in my head and I was starting to resent him for everything he was putting me through. Still I didn't leave him.

Mark had always wanted to be part of the 'cool' gang. He had been friends with Jack Tweed for a long time, so when Jack got with Jade Goody, Mark loved it. He would hang around with them all the time. I was rarely invited out with them all, but I remember the first time I got talking properly with Jade, while we were at Club 195 in Epping. It was really nice for me to be part of what I saw as Mark's 'other' life. We were just two girls chatting and gossiping about life, but the thing I remember most is her reaction to Mark. She didn't say very good things about him to me. She kept saying stuff like, 'Don't trust him – he's not good to you.' She was trying to warn me off him, but she didn't actually tell me why specifically. It made me worry even more about what was going on and what Mark might be getting up to. She said that she thought he was an arsehole and that she didn't like him being around Jack. That was the thing about Jade – she was ballsy, she said it how it was, and she had courage. People think she put up with a load of crap, but she didn't. She stood her ground, and Jack did really love her. I know that.

I'd only ever see Jade occasionally because Mark didn't include me in that part of his life. He didn't take me with him to their house. He did take me to Jack and Jade's wedding where he was best man, and I was pictured for *OK!* and ended up in the mag.

One day I saw an email that had been sent to him from the production company for *Big Brother*. It was calling him in for a meeting! It turned out a modelling agency he was connected with had put him forward. I was like, 'When were you gonna tell me you were doing that?' I think he didn't tell me because he knew I wouldn't have wanted him to do it. In the end he decided he didn't want to do it anyway. If he had, I would have probably only realised when I saw him going into the house on TV! Another time, I was reading the paper and saw Mark's picture. He was lying in bed with a girl in one of those story strips that they have in tabloids. He never told me; I just happened to stumble across it. Why was he doing this? It wasn't for the money.

I loved Mark more than I fancied him, and I couldn't care less whether he was a celebrity or not. I didn't care whether he had money or whether he had the best cars. (He always had to have a flash car.) I once told him, 'I'd rather live in a shed and be with you than be rich and famous and us not be together.' I fell in love with the real Mark, the Mark underneath it all, and I know that that Mark always loved me, no matter how he behaved. I do believe that, even though friends think I'm blinkered.

Looking back, I know that we had major trust issues right from an early stage and they eventually ate away at us as a couple. I went from being quite a strong-minded person to being a complete pushover, agreeing to everything Mark said and wanted me to do. I hung on his every word like a complete idiot. When I had reason to question him over where he'd been or something he'd done, he would sweet-talk me so easily by saying things like, 'I love you so much. You mean the world to me. I don't wanna let you go. Please think of our future. The reason I'm doing it is for my career so I can save up and get us a place.' I suspect he was just making excuses for why he had been doing stuff behind my back. It was only when he got pushed into a corner, like when that mag shoot was about to come out that he'd done with the glamour model, that he admitted anything. I made myself a doormat and he wiped his feet on me every single day. I was the mug who went back time and time again, and I'm not proud of that. I don't regret it, believe it or not, because I did love him and I know he loved me. It has shaped me as a person and has made me realise what I do want from a relationship in the future.

It's no surprise that the rows began to take over our relationship. If we weren't rowing, we were making up, and it was exhausting. We were constantly breaking up and getting back together. The rows were always over jealousy and us questioning whether one of us had been unfaithful. If I insisted that I go out, then Mark wanted me to go out with his family rather than any of my friends – like they were escorting me and checking up on me. It was quite suffocating.

Mum and Nicola didn't like the way he treated me. I would try and cover for him, because there was that side of me that loved the fact he loved me so much. I reached the point where I stopped telling my mum and Nicola about our rows or when we broke up, though, because when we got back together, it was really hard for them to accept him after what I had told them. If I told them bad things, they would start hating on him, and I didn't want that, so I ended up having no one to talk to and bottling it all up. It was knackering.

Thankfully, my new job in London helped me start to be a bit more independent. Although I would rush home to be with Mark or go out with him for dinner, it was also my first taste of being without him for a whole day! I occasionally even went for a drink after work, but Mark hated it when I did that. I started to try and have my own life a bit, and when I was nineteen, I even applied to *The X Factor*, where I got to the judges' houses, but I didn't make it through to the live shows – details on that later! For once I was enjoying myself and doing something for me.

It was just after those auditions that I got pregnant. I can remember it like it was yesterday. I could cry thinking about it because until now I have pretty much tried to block it from my mind, like if I didn't think about it, it didn't happen. That's been the easiest way to deal with it. It was a terrible time and makes me sick to think about. I hadn't seen Mark for a couple of days because of the auditions and I was due to go to Spain with Mark's sister Jessica for a family wedding, one of their cousins was getting married. Jess and I had known each other since school and were really good mates, so it was cool. Anyway, Mark and I slipped upstairs to say goodbye and that was when it happened: I got pregnant. I didn't realise until about two weeks later, of course. I knew that I was late and that something wasn't right, but I kept thinking, Surely not. I went out to buy a test while Mark waited at my mum's house for me. We sat together in the bathroom, waiting to see whether the lines came up. It was the longest two minutes ever, but finally two faint blue lines appeared. I was like, Shit – this can't be happening.

This is really strange, because I should have been terrified when I did the test, but in a weird way I felt really excited knowing that I could be carrying Mark's baby. Even so, I knew that I couldn't let myself even think about having the baby because I knew it wasn't the right time and we weren't financially stable. We didn't have a house; we had nothing. Mark was crying his eyes out – he was devastated. He was saying to me, 'I can't wait to have a baby with you in the future, but it's not right now. It's not the right time for us.' I felt that really he wasn't ready for this. I understood we weren't in the right place, but that didn't make it any easier. I remember my mum saying to me that it had to be my decision and that if I wanted to keep the baby, then that's what I should do and she would support me, but I was like, 'No, it's what me and Mark want. We aren't ready.' I think deep down, though, if Mark had said, 'Keep it,' I would have. I wanted that baby, and although I can't let my head go there, I do sometimes wonder how different my life would have been.

From that moment on I couldn't wait for us to be

more settled so we could have a family. Mark's family weren't quite so keen on the idea. When I first met him, I was envious of his family and that they were all together, but there was a part of me that always felt his mum, Carol, didn't think I was good enough. I felt she always expected the worst from me and for me to get pregnant when I was young like my mum, and so when I did, she wasn't exactly pleased about it. I felt that I'd lived up to her worst expectations.

Mark paid for me to go privately for the abortion. It was early morning and Mark drove me to a clinic in Buckhurst Hill. I was seven weeks pregnant by then, and I can remember that car journey like it was yesterday. I was trying not to think about what I was doing, but the closer we got, the worse I felt about what I was about to do. Mark and I didn't speak that much on the journey there. I think we both felt totally sh*t about what was happening. Because it was so early in the pregnancy, they gave me two tablets to bring on a miscarriage. It was hell. I took them when I got back to Mark's parents' house and they had a really bad effect on me. Almost immediately I felt terrible and started to feel sick. I was lying on the bathroom floor in Mark's parents' house sweating and crying. I was cold but pouring with sweat and was in so much pain – pain I had never felt before and have never felt since. I kept being sick because the stomach cramps were so severe. All I wanted was for Mark to hold me, I was crying out, 'Please hold me. Please hug me.' It was Carol who eventually said, 'Just hug her, Mark.' He was very emotional and I think that what we had done had really hit a nerve.

I bled a lot for the next couple of days, but I tried so hard to be strong and erase it from my mind, telling myself that it was over. It was a horrible, horrible time and I can honestly say I would never, ever do that again. Mark knew that too and he was very careful from then on because he knew that if I got pregnant for a second time, there was no way I would get rid of it. No way. We didn't speak about it again after that; it was like if we never discussed it, then it never happened.

It was something that I just did; I thought it would be selfish if I had a baby I couldn't provide for. I was just nineteen and didn't want to be a single mum. I wanted to do it the proper way. That's really important to me after my childhood. A couple of years ago I went to see a fortune-teller and she talked to me about my nanny Rose. She told me that she was holding my little boy. She said that Nanny Rose had her hand on my shoulder and was saying that she was very proud of me. She told me I would have three boys, but I'd keep going until I had a girl.

★

Mark and I moved in together in 2008, when we were twenty-two. I had already moved out of my mum's and was renting a flat, but Mark's dad had built some flats in Loughton and Mark bought one. Mark is really good with money and is not extravagant at all. He'd been saving for ages and was really chuffed that he'd managed to get his own place. I was staying around there so much that we decided that I should move in. It was lovely having a place of our own and somewhere we could call home. I loved that it was just Mark and me.

In 2010, however, our lives and our relationship changed for ever. When *The Only Way Is Essex* started, Mark and I were twenty-four and had been dating for nine years. I don't think I would have been on it if it had been left to Mark. He had already been signed up and told me I wasn't going to be part of it. When I was at the polo at Gaymes Park in Essex, though, a load of producers were there looking for people to have on the show and they pulled me to one side and did a quick interview with me on camera. When I told them my name, they had already heard of me because Mark had spoken about me, and various other local people had also mentioned me. Mark and I weren't together at the time. Just the usual for us to break up but not stop talking to or seeing each other! Because

Mark and I were on a break, I told the producers I didn't want to be involved. They insisted they wanted me for the show anyway as they wanted to portray our relationship – I guess it made good telly! I was hesitant but agreed, knowing Mark wouldn't be happy. It was a big deal for me because I was embarking on something completely different and new and I was taking a massive gamble with my life. It might be difficult to have a proper, regular job and all in the hope that the show would be a hit. It was a big decision and a scary one. I knew if it worked I would never look back but that if it didn't I'd have to start all over again in the world of 'proper' work. Thankfully it paid off.

Mark called me when he realised that I was going to be involved. 'Why do you want to leave your normal job?' he asked. 'I'll do the celeb stuff and make the money and look after you.' I was shitting myself, thinking, What am I doing agreeing to be part of something that Mark doesn't want? Mark wanted to be famous, but it felt like he just wanted me to be the little woman waiting at home for him. In some ways the idea of him looking after me was really comforting. What makes me sad is that he knew my background and my childhood; he knew my insecurities. He made me feel as though whatever he was doing was for me, but looking back it feels like it was for one person and that was Mark.

Once *The Only Way Is Essex* started, things went rapidly downhill for us. We obviously already had big issues with jealousy and trust between us, but the glare of the camera lens just seemed to magnify them. More girls were giving him attention and he liked it, and the whole thing started to take over. The scenes made good TV.

The show was a real turning point in how my family saw Mark, though. It revealed him in a very different light. My dad had been unsure of Mark at first, because he'd been worried I'd get pregnant young like my mum had, but they had grown to have a good relationship. Mark had even managed to charm him! Once Dad started to watch the show, though, he hated what he was seeing. He started to ask me why I was with him when he treated me so badly, and it became more and more awkward when he saw him.

For me, too, the show made me view Mark differently. I suddenly saw a person I didn't recognise, and I didn't like it. His player attitude was not like the Mark I knew. The show highlighted what Mark was like when I wasn't with him and he was quite a different person. I saw what he was saying and how he was behaving around other girls and I'd genuinely thought he only spoke to me like that. I found it heart-breaking ☹ Although the producers had warned me what it could be like, emotionally I was totally unprepared for it all.

When I spoke to him about it, he would just dismiss it and say it was a television show and I should ignore it. I was made to feel as though I was reading too much into things and it only added to my insecurities. It was so on and off between us anyway that my head was always in a spin, and each time it was called off, I'd be devastated. It never lasted long, though. We'd split and then hours later be talking on the phone and meeting up – we could never stay away from one another. Even when people didn't know we were together or we were supposed to have split up, on shoots we'd disappear off together without anyone knowing. It was exciting. ♥

As the show got bigger and I started to get offered work, like magazine shoots, Mark didn't like it. He liked the flat to be nice, but I was ragged trying to do all the washing and cleaning. I liked playing wife, but the more the work rolled in, the less time I had to do things and he would get really annoyed. He didn't seem to care what work I had – he seemed more interested in whether I was keeping the house clean and doing his washing.

We still continued to row all the time. We had one massive one when we were meant to be on a break. I went out with my sister Nicola and Nev, my Lauren's Way business partner – as I'd started my own company by this point – and we had a great time. Lauren Pope was there, and Maria Fowler, Lydia and Arg, but Mark was going mad that I was there. He told me that if I got drunk not to bother going home. I got caught up in it all, though, and drank and partied until 4 a.m. I finally got home at 5 a.m. and he was so cross that he wouldn't talk to me. I was like, 'I'm so sorry. Please don't ignore me.' He gave me such a hard time that I was the one apologising because I'd had a nice evening out. I felt like I was in the wrong when I wasn't. I just did what he did every weekend. For a whole day he refused to speak to me and then he finally came round and I thought, Phew! I was so relieved. I begged him to forgive me in this baby voice he liked me to put on. Yes, seriously. But he liked it, so I did it. No matter how much we rowed, we always got back together.

As the ratings for *TOWIE* soared, our work schedules became heavier and heavier. This meant we were spending less time at home and things were becoming increasingly strained between us. Then when Lucy Mecklenburgh joined the show in Series 2, things became impossible. Lucy was introduced to the show during Essex Fashion Week, where I was working. My role there was to organise everything – the venue, the collections to be shown on the catwalk and the guest list. Lucy came to see me about putting her Forever Unique clothing line on the catwalk. I had interviewed a few girls wanting their stuff shown and they'd all been really chatty, but when Lucy turned up, she acted very strangely. She just stared at me and didn't chat at all. I remember thinking it was a bit odd, and of course as things played out, I found out why. At the time, I just thought she was incredibly nervous about being on camera and so I kept saying, 'Don't worry – you're gonna be OK.' She used to turn up to filming locations with a full face of make-up on, presumably in the hope that the crew would ask her to be on the show. Mark and I were on the rocks, but we weren't properly over and I think she saw her chance.

Later that day I was in the King William IV pub in Chigwell being filmed for *TOWIE* having a quiet drink with Maria Fowler when Mark walked in with Lucy. They were clearly together. I instantly recognised Lucy from the job interview. There had been lots of talk about how Mark had met someone else when he'd been to Marbella on his own the week before, but I had no idea who until that moment. My heart started to beat really fast. It was like it was bursting out of my chest as it started to dawn on me what was happening. I began to feel panicky and like I couldn't breathe. The cameras were on me and that made it even worse, because I knew I was being watched for a reaction. I thought, I'm gonna faint. Why would he do this to me? How can he be so unkind? Very quickly, though, I started to feel angry. Tears were pricking my eyes, but I didn't want to show any weakness. It was like all my emotions were being turned upside down and magnified.

It was awful as I felt that Mark was trying to hurt me on purpose. He'd known she was coming for a job interview with me, that Essex Fashion Week was important to me. What also really got to me was the fact that she knew about me and him, because she had been watching the show, yet she had turned up for the job interview with me and said nothing, like butter wouldn't melt. I thought, She must have some f*cking front. What a liberty!

The minute I saw them, I felt sick. I was shaking all over as I went up to Mark and said to him, 'Get away from me, you absolute scumbag.' In my head it was over between us because he had moved on – he was seeing another girl. I ranted and went on and was made to look like the nutter, but do have you any idea what it feels like to see your boyfriend rock up with a new girl after so many years together? What made me even madder was the way she looked at me, like I was a piece of sh*t. She was so smug about what she had done and that's so unattractive in a girl. I thought, You don't know who I am, yet you look at me like I'm nothing. I came across like I was jealous, and as usual the one in the wrong, but there was so much I wanted to say and couldn't because the cameras were rolling.

I was upset that the producers had introduced Lucy properly to the viewers for the first time and that Mark and I had a huge fight over her. It makes good TV but it was my life. By this point my health was suffering. I was starting to feel panicky and anxious all the time. I knew I couldn't take much more. I was a f*cking laughing stock and still he managed to turn the tables and make it look like I was the mad, insecure girlfriend going crazy over nothing.

A couple of nights after, I went to Faces nightclub for Essex Fashion Week. I needed to get out and make myself feel better. Mark went there with Lucy, but at the end of the evening, Lucy realised she couldn't find Mark. She thought he must have gone outside, but Mark was really in the club with me – he'd asked the bouncer to tell Lucy he'd gone home and not to let her back in. He kept saying to me, 'I want you back. I don't like her. I want you. I'm just doing it for the storyline.' There was blatantly something going on with her, but he was trying to convince me that he wanted me. As usual I caved in, went home with him and ended up in bed with him. I look back and wonder what on earth I was thinking, but I just couldn't resist him. He was like an addiction that I couldn't kick.

Even so, I knew I'd been made to look like a mug in that pub and I wanted him to sort it out in front of the cameras so people would know that I was with him, that he wanted me and that Lucy was nothing. The night before the charity boxing match between Kirk and Mark, I stayed with him. Nobody knew we were sleeping together again; they thought he was with Lucy. We were in bed together and I told him that he needed to end it with Lucy on camera and tell the world he wanted to be with me. I knew everyone would be there, including my dad, Hayley and Jenna, and I wanted him to make things OK again. He agreed. He said to me, 'Trust me, I wanna be with you. Lucy isn't for me – she's not warm like you. She hasn't got a personality like you.' Yet again I believed him. I was so excited about going to the match and seeing him tell everyone, but he didn't do it. Lucy came up to me and confronted me, saying she knew about me and Mark going behind her back and that it disgusted her. What a bloody cheek. Instead of ending it with Lucy, Mark did the complete opposite and tried to reassure *her* that they were OK. He had no respect for anyone but himself.

I knew I needed to get away and decided that I would go to Dubai. I'd been offered a really good opportunity – a fashion job – by Adam and Simon Ryan. They are twins and the founders of Essex Fashion Week, and they have their own fashion label. My plans were cut short, however, because Mark didn't want me to go and eventually stopped me.

I think the hardest thing for me was that what he did on camera was so different to what he did off camera. He believed the storylines and played up like he was some kind of actor, but it was my life and my emotions he was playing with. It was like a form of torture.

Being around Lucy was difficult. I felt uncomfortable and it played on my insecurities. Mark should have known that and how it would make me feel. It was that control thing again. I can remember the promo video for the show and he was telling me I couldn't wear certain things because they made me look big. I was just used to him saying things like that, but it was really grating on me.

I knew it was wrong and so did everyone around me. My sister Nicola has always been so supportive of me and would always be the one I'd run to when we split up and I needed to leave the flat. One day I was chatting to her outside Switch bar in South Woodford and was moaning about him and how I couldn't see it working between us. I loved him, but it was such hard work and I'd had enough of his wandering eye. Nicola was always on my side and whenever we got back together again, she would be like, 'Are you for real? Mark is mugging you off and you're going back for more.' She liked Mark, but she saw how badly he treated me a lot of the time. Anyway, there I was outside Switch, having a moan about him, about his behaviour and how I couldn't put up with it, when Mark turned up and proposed to me there and then. I couldn't stop myself – there I was saying yes just minutes after agreeing that if I went back to him, I'd need my head read! He had a hold over me. I loved him, and we were obsessed with one another.

Though it was a dream come true when he proposed to me, I was quite shocked. Deep down I kept thinking, Is this for real? Does he mean this, or is this for TV? The emotions that I felt when Mark asked to marry me weren't what I expected. It was so weird. He must have read my mind because when the camera was off us, he whispered in my ear, 'I really mean this. It's not for the show.' You see, we weren't followed everywhere and then the footage was edited, instead we filmed actual scenes. I didn't know what was going to happen in the scenes but they were set up so a particular conversation or row or incident could be captured and would make good TV. This time, it was Mark proposing!

When Mark went to film another scene, in which he told his family that we were engaged, I had time to think about what had just happened. I thought I'd be over the moon, but instead I felt lost. I was happy – of course I was – but in the back of my mind I was asking myself, Is this the right thing to do? Am I *really* happy?

I felt trapped because I knew that I loved Mark, but I was worried whether that was enough. I felt very weird. I had always wanted to be Mark's wife, though, and regardless of my worries, my heart won out. Finally I thought he would settle down and it would just be me and him.

How wrong could I have been? In June 2011, just a couple of months after we got engaged, Mark went to Marbella and told me I couldn't go with him. I was used to that, but I still didn't like it, so I decided to go to Tenerife for a break and to take my mind off it all with an old work friend. I had a nice week, but the day I was leaving, I started to receive tweets about Mark and Lucy – something about a set of photos. People were saying that they were really sorry and felt for me. I was boarding an EasyJet flight back to London and needed to know what was going on. It was a Tuesday and all the magazines had hit the shelves. I knew in my heart that if they were together in a set of pictures, then he had done something with her – I just knew it. I thought, No sooner has he got that ring on my finger than he is cheating on me again. I started to feel like I couldn't catch my breath. I tried to get hold of him, but I couldn't, which only confirmed my fears. For the first time in my life I had a panic attack. I thought I was going to swallow my tongue. I was hyperventilating and felt like I was going to die. The stewards took me up the front of the aircraft, where they laid me down and put ice on my chest, but I was crying and in such a state. I couldn't bear what was happening and what he was doing to me. I had been so naïve to think that because we were engaged, he would change.

It seemed like the longest flight in the world. I kept imagining what Mark, my fiancé, had been up to with

Lucy and it made me feel physically sick. As soon as I got off that flight, I jumped in a cab. I was a complete mess. I was crying and asked the driver to take me to a petrol station so that I could pick up the magazine with the pictures in. It felt like ages before we found somewhere, but eventually we pulled in and I bought a copy. My heart sank when I saw them. The pictures confirmed my worst nightmares. I got back into the cab and started to cry again. I was so embarrassed and wondered what the driver must think of me, but I couldn't stop. Big, fat, hot tears were running down my face and I felt like my world had come crashing down. The cabby kept saying to me, 'Don't worry – he's not worth it, love.' He was really sweet and I think he felt sorry for me. He could see that I was in a bad way, and even when he dropped me off, he said, 'Are you sure you're OK?' I nodded, but of course I wasn't.

I was numb. It wouldn't sink in what was happening and what I'd seen, but there was Mark with his arms round Lucy in a white bikini. I was thinking, There's no way he can wriggle out of this one. As much as I tried to get hold of him, he didn't answer my calls or texts. He had flown back that the same day, though, and when I reached the flat, he was there. We barely spoke. There was no shouting or screaming, just an eerie silence between us. We didn't talk, but he could see that I was upset and said he would take me out for lunch to Sheesh in Chigwell. I went, but when I got there, I couldn't eat. I was downing wine, glass after glass, and he was like, 'Lauren, what's wrong with you?' He couldn't understand why I was so upset and he didn't seem to care how I felt. He organised a day out to try and cheer me up. He took me to Top Golf, a golfing range, and tried to make it a fun day, but I didn't enjoy it at all. I'm not sure now why I agreed to go with him in the first place; I think I was in shock. I didn't want to let go of him because I loved him, yet I knew I couldn't marry someone who could lie to me, abuse my trust and take the piss out of me in the way that he did.

That night we still hadn't talked properly. I was so upset inside, I physically hurt. I hadn't seen him for a week and part of me just wanted to cuddle him and be happy and forget about it all, but I couldn't. He kept trying to fluff over everything and act like nothing had happened, but I knew from the way he was acting that something had happened between him and Lucy. I remember I was lying in bed and he was getting ready to go out to do a PA when he came over to me, lay down next to me and took my hands. He said, 'I love you so much, but I have to tell you something. I kissed Lucy while I was away, but nothing more.'

My suspicions were confirmed. I was gutted and couldn't stop crying. He'd done it again, and while we were engaged. It hurt so much. Minutes after he told me, he walked out. He didn't care that I was beside myself. He just left to do a PA as if nothing had happened.

Lucy then sold her story, which was probably why he told me, and admitted that they had cheated together. Yet again I looked like a f*cking mug. He tweeted:

'Not allowed to say too much right now, but very shortly you'll find out the truth. "I think it happened there" – hmmm u think maybe coz it never.'

'Me and @LaurenGoodger r happy together she knows the truth anyway hope everyone has a good day.'

Although Mark had cheated on me before and I'd chosen to ignore it and stay with him, being on *TOWIE* made his behaviour public. He made me look like a mug for putting up with it. Whenever I confronted him about how he was with other girls, he'd always tell me it was just for the show and that it was a storyline and I needed to get over it. He never stopped for a minute to think how that made me feel. I was under a massive amount of outside pressure to dump him, and for the first time it started to hit me how unacceptable his behaviour really was. Now I was convinced that he was cheating on me.

I was in such a state that I called my friend Lisa. She is like a mum to me and has always been there for me. She used to do mine and my mum's hair – that's how I got to know her – but during all the difficult times in my childhood she was always there. She was a rock. Honestly, she was more like family to me than anyone else, because she listened and she got me. She knows everything I have been through and it was her I called when he left for that PA. She told me to go to her flat, which I did, and I stayed there for a few nights. She said that when I turned up, I was a nervous wreck. I lay on her hallway floor crying my eyes out. I was heaving like I was gonna be sick and she said I was struggling to catch my breath. I was a complete mess. I wanted it not to be true, but in my head I felt it was more than just a kiss. Given their history, I still suspect that he had slept with Lucy, even though to this day he denies it. Even if all they had done was kiss, at the same time he had been tweeting pictures of me saying, 'My beautiful fiancée.' How sick and disrespectful is that? Why had he bothered to ask me to marry him? Why did we have such a massively ridiculously over-the-top engagement party with him and Argent arriving on horseback if he wanted to play away? I didn't get it, and I still don't.

I tried so hard to pick myself up and put a brave face on it all. A couple of days later I went to the Lipsy launch and the press noticed that I'd taken off my engagement ring. I was wearing a white dress, and even though I tried to smile for the cameras, you can see the pain in my eyes. I was miserable.

I started to lose weight. For once I went off my food. I usually comfort-eat, but this time I couldn't eat because I was so unhappy. When I got taken on by my agent, Max Clifford, in June 2011, I barely spoke really. Any confidence I might have had was gone.

In a way, I was so low that it had become a vicious cycle: I felt crap without him and didn't believe in myself, so I just kept going back for more, and this time was no different. Of course, Mark put on his usual charm offensive and gave me all the banter and I so desperately wanted to believe him. He would try and make me feel really special by hugging me and kissing me and taking me out, and somehow he would turn it all round on me so that I didn't know what to believe. Even with the facts staring me in the face, he would make me believe that the pictures were wrong or that the story was inaccurate. He could talk his way out of anything and I was blinded by my love for him.

He took me to Marbella, but it was strained. He had a PA to do and needed to come back a day early. He didn't want me staying out there on my own, but his sister Jess was there and she told him to stop being ridiculous, so he agreed. He gave me such a hard time about staying, yet if I'd gone back, I'd have just been going back to an empty flat. I tried really hard to put the whole Lucy thing to the back of my mind and get on with it.

We went to Vegas that June to celebrate our engagement and I hoped that it could be a fresh start. We had first-class tickets and were like a couple of kids in a sweetshop, we were so excited. It was the first holiday we have ever had where we went out clubbing as a couple and didn't row! I even had a drink with him and he didn't mind. It was amazing and I really believed that things were going to be different. We bought a video camera and took some really sweet footage of the two of us. Best of all, we were having fun. I've got a load of pictures of us out there, and despite the press saying we looked miserable, we really weren't – we had a great time and spent every day relaxing by the pool. The only fly in the ointment was that Mark spoke to his parents at least once a day. That was quite normal for Mark, but I thought it was a bit weird. When you're on holiday with your fiancé, you don't really expect him to be on the phone to his parents, do you? Often I would feel as though there was both Mark and Mark's family in our relationship because they knew our every move – where we were, what we were doing . . . It was strange.

When we got back from Vegas, things started to slip back to normal, and instead of feeling happy, I started to feel trapped and suffocated. Mark was out all the time doing PAs and I was stuck at home, just as he liked. I was so lonely I bought a dog. I didn't ask Mark, because I knew he would say no, so I just brought him home and hoped he wouldn't go too mad. He was furious, of course. He was like, 'Lauren, you need to get rid of that dog. We're not keeping him.' I was determined, though, and eventually he agreed. He was a little Chihuahua and we named him Wrighty! He was company when Mark wasn't there, and I got really attached to him. So did Mark in the end, and if he ever went away, he used to cry about leaving the dog. I thought it was quite sweet, but it was actually a bit odd.

The excitement and fun in our relationship had gone and I was like a bored housewife. The house was immaculate, the washing was done, and I was sitting pretty waiting for Mark to come home. Sometimes I'd go to see Jess, Mark's sister, to get me out of the house, but most of the time it was me and Wrighty.

Just a few months after Mark kissed Lucy in Marbella, he dropped the bombshell that he was going to Marbella again. He had promised me that he would never do that again, after what had happened. What's worse is the way he did it. I remember he told me while we were filming the promo for the third series of *TOWIE*. He was wearing a fat suit at the time. He had been really horrible to me all day while we were filming and kept putting me down; then he told me just as we were about to film a scene. I told him he had to book me a flight too, but he was like, 'No, Lauren, it's for work. You are staying here.' I felt sick and like my insides were burning, but I had to carry on and film. It was awful.

Straight after filming, he upped and left for Marbella, and I had to deal with it. The next day was the naked shoot with *Heat* magazine and I was feeling really upset. I didn't want it to show too much. I was so angry with Mark for what he had done that when he phoned me while I was being interviewed, I was really offish. It was like I loved him, but I hated him at the same time. While all that was going on with him, I had to take my clothes off and reveal all my insecurities. It was hard. I hated those pictures – who wouldn't? After the shoot I had a few glasses of wine and decided if Mark was out having fun, then why wasn't I? So I went out that night with my friend Lynsey.

Little did I know that decision would have such dramatic consequences. I went to Aura and someone told Mark I had cheated. It was complete bull sh*t, but the next day he told me to get out. And that was it – it was over. I didn't even fight it this time. I'd had enough. I moved into Lauren Pope's place because she had a spare room, and Mark's spokesperson put out a statement saying, 'It is true Mark has split with Lauren and asked her to move out of his flat two days ago.' I was like, Are you for real? I was never unfaithful to Mark, but because he believed some boy's word over mine, he ended it all. It was ridiculous.

I was being accused of cheating and was upset that it had come to an end, but at the same time in a strange way I felt quite free. Mark, my security blanket, wasn't there any more, but I wasn't as distraught as I had been on previous occasions.

The press had a field day and lots of untrue things were published about me. It was an awful time. I went to Alec's Restaurant, Bar & Grill in Brentwood that Sunday evening and during the meal I had a panic attack. It was so bad that I had to be taken upstairs to lie down. I was hyperventilating and couldn't catch my breath. The manager could see what was happening and managed to get me upstairs and away from everyone else in the restaurant. I can barely remember the room, but I was laid on a sofa. He was trying to calm me down, but I couldn't breathe. My arms had gone numb and I thought I was having a heart attack. I was so frightened and kept thinking, Please don't let me die. I don't want to die.

I think I was upstairs for about an hour before I started to feel more normal and was able to get myself home. Anyone who has suffered from a panic attack will know how awful and how frightening it is. No words can properly describe the fear I have when I have an attack.

I felt so humiliated to know the whole country had seen my boyfriend mess about with other girls. I worried there might have been other girls I didn't know about, but another one I did find out about, in the most horrible way possible, was the snog with Sam Faiers in October 2011. Mark and Sam had a history which made it even harder to deal with. Even now I don't know everything that happened between them but Mark had seen a bit of her when we were teenagers. We had lots of breaks and it may have been during one of those breaks but I really don't know and in a way it doesn't matter because it still happened. Seeing them together upset me more than ever because of that. It made me think about them together 'properly' and it made me feel sick. We had not long split up from our engagement, but I was missing him and in my head I wanted to get back with him. Even at that point 'off' never really meant off. That's how it was with us. It was Halloween and one of the producers told me that I needed to run through this bush with Lauren. We both ran through wondering what was waiting for us. I never in a million years thought it would be Mark kissing Sam. I could see them together and I started crying and stormed off. I ripped off my mic and wanted to go home, but the producers hadn't got the right shot, so they asked me to do it again. I was so upset, but I felt I should do it. I was crying and screaming. I couldn't believe they had made me watch that, knowing how devastated I'd be after having broken up with Mark so recently. I was in absolute bits that night. I couldn't believe he had done it. I thought it was so disrespectful, of both of them.

Mark and I never moved back in together, but just a couple of weeks later we were talking again and meeting up in secret. It seems mad now to think what I was willing to put up with. As usual, he talked me round, and I just couldn't give him up. He told me Sam meant nothing. The thing with Sam was awful at the time, but I somehow got my head around it and tried to forget how badly he'd treated me when our engagement had been called off.

No one knew we were back together. We stayed in so no one would see us, and when I stayed at Mark's, I'd be really careful to check that no paparazzi were following me. Then I'd park my car a few streets down so we wouldn't get rumbled. If he drove me to my flat that I started renting after I moved out of Lauren's he'd drop me at the nearby petrol station. It was all about making sure that we avoided getting pictured together, because he didn't want us to go public. The press thought we had split, and in interviews we said that we didn't speak any more, but we did.

I remember I was his last phone call before his mobile got taken away and he went into the jungle when he did *I'm a Celebrity . . . Get Me Out of Here!* in November 2011. He told me how much he loved me and told me not to worry about anything that happened in there because it was for a TV show. When he came out, though, he didn't call me. I was in Lapland filming for *The Only Way Is Essex* and had been busy so hadn't watched the whole series and wondered whether he had got with someone while he was in there. I felt sick because I knew something was wrong. Not ringing me was a signal something was up. It was a few days before we finally spoke and it was like his success had gone to his head. Don't get me wrong – he had done really well, but it was as if he thought he was gonna be some kind of movie star. It was then that he told me that while he was in there, he'd got over me and realised he didn't love me any more. It was like a rollercoaster of emotions for me. One minute he loved me, the next he didn't. It was so hard. Our relationship became very odd over this period. I thought that we would be back together but he didn't think so. This was later played out in the press, so you've all read about it, but it was very upsetting for me.

Mark went to America to film *Mark Wright's Hollywood Nights*. Little by little I started to enjoy not having him around. I was glad he wasn't in the country. I could do what I wanted. Though I still felt very lost, I knew I needed to get on with my life and I loved the freedom. I even went to Marbella for the first time on my own, which was a very big decision for me, and it was wicked. I was there at boot camp which was hard-core, but afterwards I stayed on in Marbella with the girls and I think it was the best holiday of my life. Everyone thought I was single and I got a lot of attention from the boys, which helped me regain some confidence. I got up every day without having this sinking feeling, wondering what sort of mood Mark was in.

We saw each other when he came back, but it was horrible. The fun had gone and I was nervous to go to his flat because of how he might be. One evening I went over to the flat after a night out. It wasn't the same – something had gone. I realised that I had been happier when he was in America. Our relationship had become a battleground. I thought, How can I win? I'd had enough. It was all so tedious and demoralising. For the first time I realised it wasn't love; it was obsession.

We both knew it was over. And you know what? I feel free. I actually feel amazing. I dream about Mark – weird things like sleeping with him, seeing him – but I think they are memories. I can't cut them out of my life. It's still relatively raw and fresh. I don't sit and pine, though. I get up and go out. I don't wallow and I'm getting on with my life and moving on. There are days when I feel a bit sh*t, but I don't wanna mope around. I wanna show him that I can survive on my own and that I won't let him get to me anymore.

Looking back now, I recall that every morning of those last few days of being with him, I'd wake up with a pain in my chest, like a panicky feeling because I was worried about what he was gonna say to me. Once we broke up, that feeling went. I wake up happy now. It's like a weight has lifted from my shoulders. Strangely,

I felt quite relieved that I wasn't having to sit in that bloody flat on my own any more.

To be honest, it's still quite hard for me to talk about all of this, because the last thing I want to do is give him an opportunity to say that I am using his name to further my career, when I have actually had more work since we split up. But also the truth is that no matter what Mark has done, I have always been quite soft and given him the benefit of the doubt. He was my world, and even now, after everything, it's hard for me to admit what it was really like between us. I continually feel like I want to make excuses for him, which I know is wrong, but I can't help it. As much as I hate what he says about me and how convincing his lies were, I still don't want to hurt him. I've got no interest in hurting him.

Deep down I know that Mark will always love me and that he will always have a special place in his heart for me, even if he never admits it. When we split, he was always in bits. It's just nobody saw that – you only ever saw him looking like he didn't give a sh*t. I wanted me and Mark to be forever. I really did love him, more than normal love – I loved every part of him, the good and the bad. We were so close and he was my rock through hard times. We grew up together and we always ended every phone call before we went to sleep with 'Good night, love you loads more than anything in the world'. If we didn't say it right he would make us say it again and I would always have to be the one to say 'in the world' last. If I could have had my fairytale then we would have stayed engaged, got through the hard times and people against us. I don't think he fought hard enough in the end but I can't regret that because I'm a true believer in what will be, will be. He will always have a place in my heart and one thing I can never forget is that he made my heart feel true love and I know when I die I will die knowing I felt the feeling of true love.

I don't know why he hasn't just been civil. We bumped into each other recently, in Mojoes in November 2012. That was the first time we'd seen each other since our split. Although we only live down the road from one another, we had managed to avoid each other until that point. It was so weird because he knew full well I was going to be there, because Mojoes had tweeted it, and yet he went anyway. He then stood by my table with his back to me. When I saw him, I have to admit I felt really weird. I'm sure anyone who bumps into an ex would feel the same, but my heart did race and I felt a bit sick. Not because I fancied him or wished we were together – it was just because it caught me by surprise, I didn't know he was going. It made me feel sad that he could barely even look at me. I was engaged to him and spent most of my life with him, and I thought, Does that count for nothing? Perhaps our past does mean nothing to him now, and being so defensive and denying that we were seeing each other is his way of moving on and dealing with it, but I find that strange. Perhaps he is being told by someone to behave like this, or he is protecting his ego because this time I *have* actually moved on and for once I don't want him back.

I just wish he had a bit more respect for me and could at least recognise me as a friend. How hard would it be for him to say that we were friends and that we talk as friends? We were together for a long time and I wish things had ended differently. Instead he spends his time denying that we were even in contact, when we were. That's what hurts me the most, I think.

You know what, though? He's done me a favour because I will never put up with crap like that ever again.

It makes me sad that it's turned out the way it has. I feel like I've loved and lost, and like I have been through more than some people have by the time they are forty! I still believe he is my soul mate, and irrespective of him doing things I don't agree with, I don't regret our past. Will I get back with him? No. I certainly have no plans to or any desire to, but in all honesty there are days when I worry that I won't find anyone I have a connection with like I did with Mark. He's the only proper boyfriend I have had and I don't know any different. After everything he's done, though, I know a miracle would have to happen. If it was still the same Mark I loved, then it would be different, but I can't see it and besides someone else is in my life now and I'm pretty loved up!

It's still early days and part of me doesn't want to be tied down but last November I started dating Jake McClean. We have known each other for a while but just to say hi to and that – nothing more. He started to follow me on Twitter and when I followed him back, he direct messaged me and we decided to meet up. Within four days we were boyfriend and girlfriend – it just felt so right and it honestly feels like we have been together forever. At the time of writing this book we haven't spent a day apart from one another and I'm hoping it will stay that way, but I don't want to say too much in case I jinx it! At the moment it feels really easy and there is a real connection between us.

Our first date was at the cinema – we went to see *Breaking Dawn*. Straight away I felt comfortable with him and totally at ease. That week we saw each other loads and just really enjoyed each other's company. I think he's hot and has an amazing body but I don't want to give him a big head! Lol. Who knows where it will end up – I am just enjoying my time with him.

He's really cool and we have a laugh together. I like it that he's not famous and he handles the whole fame thing really well. When we were invited to Katie Price's New Year's Eve Party he wasn't star struck and that was really refreshing to see. He takes everything in his stride. He is such a gentleman and treats me like a princess - opening doors for me and walking on the closest side to the road. I've never really been treated like that before. He never lets me pay for a thing no matter how much I insist and is always surprising me with presents like pink trainers to match his! Maybe a part of me is worried about getting myself properly tied down again so soon but I'm having a really good time and I don't want it to end.

When we first got together Jake told me about his past. He was upfront from the word go. I had an idea anyway as he is from my area and I knew of him. As much as I was initially shocked, I could see how much he regretted his actions and how sorry he was. Everyone makes mistakes and Jake served his time for his. If he could turn back the clock, he would in a second. I try to take people as I find them. Jake is so lovely with me and he makes me smile and feel confident in myself and that's what matters to me. What happened in Jake's past is exactly that – in his past. He was young and made a huge mistake. But he has paid for it and I respect that.

Since I have been with him the feelings I had for Mark have finally disappeared and I think I needed something like this to happen in order to finally move on. I don't see Mark in the same way anymore and I see him as part of my past and not my future. It is so important for me to find myself again and Jake is allowing me to do that. My relationship experience has made me a stronger person and I am a great believer in everything happening for a reason. I don't regret falling in love and for a while I worried that I would never feel like that again but I think I can. I will always cherish the memories I have with Mark but that chapter of my life is over and it's time for a new one to begin. Love isn't a destination, it's a journey. This Valentine's Day will be my first without Mark and hopefully my first with Jake – I know he will plan something really special and I can't wait!

Apart from Jake, the only person I have spent any real time with since Mark is Tom Pearce. He asked me out while I was still seeing Mark, so I said no, but when we split up for good and Tom asked me out again, I thought, Why not? It felt weird and a bit scary going on a date with someone other than Mark. I suppose that's natural after all this time, but it was odd. I got papped with Tom pretty quickly, and straight away Mark tweeted something about it. It's like no matter how much I try to move on, Mark likes to pass comment and judgement on what I do. He did the same when I went to Marbella last May partly for a holiday and partly because I went to a weight loss boot camp and he tweeted, 'This is something you're gonna regret for the rest of your life. Yes, regret.' If he doesn't care, why is he bothering to tweet about me?

I always thought that I could never go out with any of the other boys on *The Only Way Is Essex*, and although I was hanging around Tom, I didn't think anything would happen. He liked me before he came on the show and would always be around me because he thought I was different in reality. He thought I was funny and a laugh. Then I started to worry that he was only interested in me to get a good storyline. I was becoming paranoid. In a way, going out with Tom was the first step towards showing that I was moving on from Mark, but it didn't feel right. When I was drunk, I fancied him, but when I wasn't, I felt nothing.

I like a certain type. I like the loudest, the sexiest, the good-looking one, but I didn't feel like I fancied Tom enough. I wasn't ready and I think I need to be single for a while and go wild and live the teenage years that I never really had. He is a sweet guy and would always stand up for me, though. He said that I was perceived in the wrong way and that he had my back. I think he genuinely cared for me as a person. It lasted about a month with Tom, and in that time we went on a few dates, to Sheesh restaurant and to Faces nightclub. We had a nice time, but I didn't feel the spark. He seemed a bit young – he was twenty-three, so three years younger, and little things about him annoyed me, like his nostrils and his eyebrows! He talks with his eyebrows – they like move around all the time and it is really distracting! And he was a bit of a worrier, which I don't find attractive. He was a great kisser, though, and that made me fancy him a bit, but he had no swagger or coolness about him. I like a smart bad boy like Jake.

When I finished it, I was asked to do it on camera, which was really awkward, and I did that whole 'it's me, not you' thing that the guys usually do. He got the hump and didn't want to speak to me. I didn't want to fall out with him, but I think he found it easier to cut ties. It took about three months before he messaged me and said he missed me. I told him I missed him too, but it was in a mates' way, nothing more. It was fun, but it was no great love affair. I think on the show it looked like Lauren Pope was really pissed off with me, but in fact she was a really good friend to me. Tom and Lauren had been on a few dates, but that was it. We have never fallen out over Tom. She never wanted him, and I wouldn't have done it if she had her sights set on him. It was nothing.

I think my brief relationship with Tom really wound up Mark, though. I was in Faces one night when Jermain Defoe had a table and there were a few of us having a great time. Then Mark showed up and I was told there was a fuss about me being there. The first I knew of what had happened was when I got called over by the manager, who told me, 'I'm really sorry, Lauren, but Mark is here and it's a bit awkward, so it's best if you go.' I was utterly furious. I was like, 'There will be no trouble. We are all on a table here spending loads of money and you are kicking me out?' He wouldn't back down, though, so off I went. I was so upset that Mark might feel like that and the club were prepared to ask me to leave. It was a bloody joke.

Things like that really sadden me because Mark is very popular and I worry that I'll get turned away from clubs or kicked out again. I was so embarrassed that night as I got my bag and left. It was awful, and not only was I hurt, I was also furious that this could happen. When I got home, I broke down in tears.

Mark rang me the next day to apologise. He said, 'Lauren, you've got a new boyfriend now and I don't want to be in the same club as you.' I went mental at him, telling him exactly what I thought. Not that it made any difference – Mark is never going to change. #selfish

And for a while I went really wild – going out all the time. I felt like I had missed out on so much and that finally I was able to have fun. I wasn't trying to prove anything and I'm still not.

What scares me most about dating again is starting from the beginning. I was worried because Mark knows everything about me and everything I've been through. He saw how I was with my mum and dad. He was the one who used to pick me up if I had a blazing row with Mum in the middle of the night, and I find it hard to imagine being that close to someone else, although I think it's starting to happen! I used to get worried that other blokes would have seen *The Only Way Is Essex* and think that I'm some jealous nutter or something. It's embarrassing. I would worry about things like, What if I don't have the same banter with another bloke as Mark and I did? What if I can't find someone to love me for me? Those are genuinely things I used to worry about. It's not been easy but I'm getting there, and when I do regain my confidence, I know that I will never look back.

Right now I need to concentrate on having fun and not worry about anything else, but that's hard. Time is ticking and my biggest achievement in life will be when

I start a family. If I was asked what I want for my future, there is only one thing I am sure of. I want to be married for life with no cheating, a heap of trust, five kids and a big house. Lol. For me, that's my dream. I'd give it all up tomorrow for that. ☺

My Dating Rules

1. Be classy.

2. Be cute but flirty.

3. Be confident but not arrogant. I find it really hard to go up to guys and talk to them, but sitting in the corner never gets you a date.

4. A drink might help you calm your nerves, but don't drink too much – it's not attractive and you won't remember what you got up to the next day.

5. Enjoy that nervous feeling – it won't last for ever.

If you want something serious, don't go home with him – just swap numbers. ☺

4

The Pressure to Be Thin

I LOVE FOOD. There, I have said it. I love food. Is that so wrong? If I were to believe half of the articles I read, then yes, apparently it is wrong. Very wrong! In this business it seems as though it's a sin to enjoy a meal, and I'm not gonna lie – that's something I find really difficult to deal with. I find it quite hard when everything I eat is documented and my weight is examined on what feels like a daily basis. I think any girl would, however happy she was in herself.

I have never been thin like Lauren Pope, but then again I have never wanted to be. You can imagine the size difference between us when we stand next to each other, though. It's enough to make anyone feel big! I enjoy feeling like a woman and having curves, and I think it's the wrong message to send out being that thin.

In a funny way, I feel proud and that I shouldn't change, because I represent so many women out there. To me, being skinny is not sexy. Take Victoria Beckham – I would never want to be that thin. Each to their own, but I much prefer the body of Beyoncé, who has great curves and a more womanly figure. This is a bit of a contradiction, but I do also love some of the Victoria's Secret models' bodies. I know a lot of them are tiny, but there are some who are curvier than others. They are slim, but they also have some shape and I'd love to look like them – they look amazing – but that's never gonna happen! As much as I want it, I don't have the discipline to get my body even vaguely like them. I think most men prefer women with a bit of shape, like Mark – he said he loved my curves and that skinny women were a complete turn-off for him. I would hate to be skin and bone. I think it's really unattractive, and I genuinely think blokes do too.

If you asked me to describe myself, I'd say that I think I am girly, feminine, glamorous, curvy, sexy and classy, and that's how I like it. Having said that, I would be lying if I didn't admit that I do feel massive outside pressure to look a certain way and to lose weight, and it's dominated my thoughts for a while now.

Even before I was in the limelight, I was quite body-conscious, but I was also fairly confident with my curves, or at least I didn't obsess about what I was eating or worry that everyone was judging me. Now I'm in the public eye, though, it's like the world is watching my every move – including everything I eat – and that has definitely knocked my confidence. The body fascists love nothing more than to have a go at me at every available opportunity, which is hard. I'm not a naturally skinny person and it feels like the older I'm getting, the bigger I'm getting, or maybe that's the pressure around me that's making me feel like that.

Although I'm in love with the idea of being curvy, and I really don't want to be skinny, the temptation to lose weight and avoid the flak is very appealing. A part of me would love to disappear and then come back having lost a heap of weight and be really skinny. I'd love to know what people would say. In reality, though, I know that if I went back to that now, I'd probably look a bit ridiculous, and instead of getting 'fat' jibes, I'd probably get targeted for looking bony or something. I know I'll never be able to win. I can understand why so many celebrities go that way. When you're punished for the way you look, like I am on a daily basis, it makes you very paranoid. I'm basically punished because I want to eat more than a lettuce leaf a day. Ahhhh, it makes me so angry!

I feel sad that my weight has started to dominate my thoughts and is permanently on my mind. I spend my life worrying about what other people will think of me and I'm always trying to avoid the hateful messages people post about me. I'd like to think I'd be able to stick two fingers up at the haters, and at first I did, but at times I've felt really bullied by them and like I can never get away from it. It's hard not to believe the crap they're writing.

I have been bullied before, not badly but enough to know that it's bloody horrible when people start on you. I was at school when I got picked on and it was only ever girls who bothered. I was popular and had a lot of friends, but when I got with Mark, a lot of the girls were really jealous and used to start on me. It was always bitchy comments. And here I am at twenty-six still being bullied. Now it's for the way I look, or my weight, or my behaviour. Bullies always find something to get at you over. The trick is not to let them bother you. I try and block out all the nasty comments and think, It's OK that I'm curvy. That's a good thing. But that's hard to do, especially when they call me all sorts of names, like a 'beached whale', a 'fat c*nt' and 'Miss Piggy'. One person said I was the sperm my mum should have swallowed. People can be so abusive when they are hiding behind a computer and I don't think they realise the hurt they cause, or maybe they do and that's what they get their kicks from. It's just plain nasty.

The trouble is, though, their comments don't encourage me to lose weight; they make me go the other way. When

I'm upset, I eat; I don't starve myself like some girls. I comfort-eat, and I have no willpower – if I fancy a plate of chips, I'll have a plate of chips. If I fancy a sandwich, I'll have a sandwich. I crave carbs and bad food, and I'm honest about that. I don't suppose many people would admit that, but that's me, that's who I am. I eat to make myself feel better and then I get even more sh*t from people. In my head, it's like everyone is pointing the finger at me and saying, 'You're fat.' It's hideous. Sometimes, when I'm feeling really low, I just want to hide away so no one can have a go at me. People should feel ashamed of making another human being feel like that.

Since the start of *The Only Way Is Essex* I have become more paranoid about my weight and how I look. I could barely watch the first series, mainly because of how Mark was but also because of how I thought I looked. I could definitely never watch it on my own in case I saw something that upset me, and I would shake when I watched it. Although there was a *TOWIE* therapist on hand I was not yet able to verbalise what was really wrong. I felt so ashamed and I started to take herbal calming tablets. It was ridiculous. I miss the time when I could chuck on anything and it would look good. I miss the time when I didn't worry about covering everything up.

This time last year I was definitely bursting out of curvy. I was much bigger than I am now and was desperate to shift some weight. I knew I wasn't fat, but everything was feeling tight. I started to avoid mirrors, and if I did catch a glimpse, I would see a girl who needed to lose weight. I never thought that I was fat, but I wasn't comfortable with myself. A night out was one of the rare times when I did look in the mirror to check that I was happy with how I looked. I wouldn't have gone out if I thought I looked horrible, but always, always the pap pictures the next day looked awful. The day after the night before, I wanted to cry because I knew the worst pictures of me would have been chosen. When I looked in the mirror before I left the house, I didn't look like the person in the pictures. It happens all the time, even now, and I always look so much bigger than I really am. I don't know, I can't work it out, but sometimes I think they deliberately choose the worst picture they can find of me and that any decent ones get chucked. I only say that because when I was on holiday in Marbella last year, I was so conscious the whole time about my body that I tried to cover up as much as possible and they still laid into how I looked, but I have got pictures on my phone of me on that same holiday in a bikini and I look completely different. I suppose a story about me looking really good won't do the same for sales.

Often when I see nasty photos of myself, I'm like, 'How can I think I look good and then a picture of me like that is taken?' and suddenly I hate myself. ☹ Half the time I can't believe it is the same person I was looking at in the mirror the night before. I saw that someone agreed the other day. They commented on some pictures of me and said, 'What she sees in the mirror and what we see are two different things.' They were being mean, but they are right – I do see something different. Maybe I have some kind of body dysmorphia. Most people look in the mirror and see someone fatter, but I see someone slimmer.

Every time I go out, I make sure I am really happy with the way I look and then the next day when I look at my iPhone, I see pictures of myself that I barely recognise. People send me links to the articles, so it's hard to avoid them. I'll be on a high because I've had a great night out and then I see those pictures and they stop me in my tracks. It's horrible. I hate the idea of people thinking I am a really big girl when I'm not. The *Daily Mail* online is the cruellest and most judgemental of me. At the end of last year I had really had enough. I felt bullied and thought twice about going out because I didn't want to be pictured. I started to not tweet where I was going so that I couldn't be pictured. I don't think they can realise the effect it has on me.

The articles can be so mean too – like when I was basically being compared to Gemma Collins and they said we had squeezed ourselves into skin tight outfits. But they had chosen pictures in which I looked really big. The Internet comments were particularly unkind. One of them said, 'Two overstuffed sausages.' It just feels unfair because I'm genuinely not as big as they make out. I'm actually often stopped by people in the street who say to me that they can't believe how small I really am. It was nice not so long ago when I saw a post standing up for me underneath an article saying I looked bad. It said, 'This is super harsh. She crash-dieted because of articles like this, putting herself in danger. Stop giving this girl a complex!' And that's exactly what I have got – a complex over how I look.

I remember one comment posted by someone under an article about an unflattering outfit I was wearing. It read, 'Vile fat pouty trouty pig . . . or is that duck . . . just stay in love u stink of desperation.' This person doesn't even know me – they are just some horrid Internet troll. However strong a person I am, those sorts of comments get to me. I think if they didn't, I would be someone without any feelings, whereas I take things to heart. I dwell on everything for longer than I should and let things get to me and upset me. I have to learn to try and let it wash over me.

When people really have a go at me, I try hard to put things into perspective. I remind myself how lucky I am. When I was twenty-one, for instance, I had a cancer scare. I went for my usual routine smear test and they found abnormal cells. I had fallen out with my mum at the time, I'd moved out, and we weren't talking, but thank God she phoned me to tell me that I had some post. It was that that got us talking again. If she hadn't, things could have been very different. The letter said that the test had shown up some abnormal cells and that I needed to have a colposcopy, a procedure where they look at what's going on and then treat it. When I read that letter, my heart sank and the first thing that I thought was, I'm gonna die. I've got cancer. I was frightened about what they might find and I was nervous about the procedure.

Although Mark and I were on a break at the time, I told him what was happening and I think he spoke to his mum, who said it was quite common in women, and he told me not to worry. Because we weren't together, my good friend Lisa took me to the Princess Alexander Hospital in Harlow and waited while I had it done. It was quite painful even though they gave me a local anaesthetic, and afterwards I bled for a while and felt weak. In my case, they were able to laser the abnormal cells away. I was so relieved that it was over, but I worried for ages that it hadn't gone away and that something bad was going to happen to me. I had to go back every six months for a smear test. Now I just have one yearly, and, thank God, it all seems to be clear. So many girls don't get themselves checked and think it only happens to older people, but I was just twenty-one when that happened.

The really weird thing is that Nicola, my sister, had the same thing two weeks later, and it turns out that my mum also had abnormal cervical cells when she was younger. Thankfully, we have all been treated and it hasn't returned, but it's always at the back of my mind. So when the bullies are at their worst, thinking about what happened makes me realise how small-minded they really are.

When I moved out of Mark's the year before last my post was still going there and a doctor's letter came through to remind me that I needed to have a smear. Knowing I'd had problems in the past, Mark called me to tell me I needed to go. We weren't together, but he bothered to ring me and remind me. That's the caring side of Mark. He could be a real sh*t at times, but the other side was very protective of me.

I might be happy with having some curves, and I genuinely don't want to be up and down, but I've definitely got a lot of insecurities about my body. I think most girls do. It's just mine are highlighted on a daily basis and very publicly, which is embarrassing.

The constant articles and picking up on my weight and what I am wearing have really started to get to me now. I find it embarrassing as much as anything. Who else from *TOWIE* has their weight discussed every time they go out? No one. I find it so frustrating because there is nothing I can do to stop it. The only chance I get to say anything and defend myself is via Twitter. People probably think that I earn a good living and that it's a small price to pay, but money's not everything. The constant weight debate and criticism about the way I dress get on my nerves. I thought it might have got better once I left the show, in August 2012, but it hasn't. I'm tired of it all. I try so hard not to let them beat me, and I'm determined that they won't, but in the early days it was tough and I have to admit a few times the comments did make me cry. I've had just about enough now and I don't know how to make it stop.

I can remember last November I went on a night out and felt really nice. I thought I looked classy and attractive, but the next day I woke up to a barrage of hate on the *Daily Mail* online. The photographer who'd papped me had literally jumped out on me from some bushes as I'd left my flat and I'd closed my eyes because the flash went off at such close range. I told him to leave me alone and that he was on private property, but he didn't listen and then a few hours later that set of awful pictures turned up of me. The *Daily Mail* website can be so hateful and judgemental. It's easy to say just ignore it, but I can't all of the time.

Instead I try and focus on the nice stuff people say – like when fans write to me saying that I've helped them feel okay about themselves, or that my story has inspired them. Sometimes they say really lovely things about how I look and that sort of thing makes me smile and realise that not everyone thinks I'm minging, which really means something to me. When I'm rational about it all, I know that most girls do like how I dress. Hybrid tell me that every time I wear one of their dresses, it sells out everywhere and that to me proves that girls do like to copy my style and that the haters are in the minority. If I think about that, it makes me feel a whole lot better about things.

If it's not my body being criticised, then I've noticed that the press love a picture of me eating, the suggestion being that all I do is stuff my face. There's one picture that I absolutely hate, and at the time it really upset me. It was early morning and we were filming *The Only Way Is Essex* and were all having breakfast. I had no make-up on and was helping myself to a bacon roll like everyone else. A paparazzi photographer pictured me eating it and the picture went everywhere. It was awful. I was so embarrassed I wanted to cry. I was branded a 'pig' and the captions, headlines and public's comments that went with the picture were so cruel that I wanted to curl up in a ball and not go out for a week. It was like I had been singled out and picked on because I'm not stick-thin. I am an average girl and face the battle with those few extra stubborn pounds like everyone else.

Oh my God, I have cried over pictures I have seen of myself. There were some pictures of me in a bikini and I was slumped over so you could see rolls round my tummy. Even the thinnest of people when they lean over can have a roll, but with me it was picked up and printed everywhere. I think it was the time when Mark and I went to Vegas and were having a good time. It brought me down straight away and I thought, I've had enough. From then on I dreaded going away and what pictures might be being taken. I'm quite vulnerable and I do feel sh*t about myself a lot of the time, so the pictures play on that and make me worry about things even more. There have been times when I've not gone away because I don't want the pressure of knowing everyone is watching and waiting to get that awful picture. When I went to Marbella a couple of months later, I wore lots of kaftans and long tops so that no one could see my body, which pissed me off because it's not like I'm obese. I just wasn't prepared to risk it.

When I have a good day, I don't care about it, but it's those low days when my insecurities are exposed that it gets to me. I feel fat one minute, sexy the next, and then I see a picture of myself and hate myself all over again.

Whenever I'm out, I'm thinking about how I'm standing so my legs don't look fat or how my face is tilted so that my face doesn't look fat, because I know that one false move and a bad picture is taken. There have been times when I have hidden myself away to eat something because I can't bear the idea of another hideous picture of me and all the nasty troll comments that go with it.

It's funny because I receive a lot of fan mail and not one has ever been nasty about the way I look. In fact, it's the complete opposite. People are incredibly supportive of me, and although when it's happening it doesn't feel like it, I know it is the minority who are unkind and judgemental. I'd like to know what they look like. One letter, sent to my agent, really touched me:

Hi Max,

I am writing to you because I am fed up of seeing nega-tive comments about Lauren Goodger and what she wears in the press.

Lauren is a gorgeous girl with a gorgeous curvy figure and she's a great role model to young impressionable girls who think thin is the way to be. Lauren is a healthy and attrac-tive size and that is what girls should be aspiring to be.

When the press write pieces on Lauren wearing an unflat-tering dress, 'getting it wrong again' or 'squeezing herself' into a tight dress, this is not only upsetting for Lauren, but it is also having a negative effect on the young girls who look up to her.

Kind regards,

Sian Miller

People probably think that I'm quite gobby. On the show, I was always the one portrayed like that, but I'm actually a very nervous person. I get scared a lot and worry about everything. Even going to the shops on my own makes me feel panicky, so I wait until a mate comes over. I have been like that for a long time; in fact, when I was younger, Mum made me go and see a therapist about it because I was scared of doing anything by myself. I don't know why, but at one stage I had this irrational fear that if I went out alone, I'd be kidnapped, which is ridiculous. The therapist said I would grow out of it, but I haven't and I still find the idea of going anywhere on my own really daunting. Very recently I have started to get into cabs on my own, but that's a battle because I worry about dodgy cab drivers. If I go to a foreign country, I can never leave the hotel alone to go to the shops; someone has to come with me. It's like I think someone is going to abduct me, or I hate the idea of some weird man bibbing me as I walk down the road.

Even the thought of someone I don't know coming over and speaking to me makes me start to panic. I'm trying really hard to deal with it at the moment, and getting into cabs is the first step. Lol. I still hate it, but I am making myself. I think it's just a weird insecurity; the idea of being alone frightens me. This is the kind of thing I've had to try and get over, and all the while I was seeing Mark, which I know now was another unhealthy situation. Often we would finish scenes late at night and I'd have to go home to an empty house and it would freak me right out. I hated it.

Even now I'll usually get a mate to stay with me, or I'll go over to their house because I hate being on my own so much. If I knew I had to go home alone, I would find myself starting to panic at the thought and would get myself all worked up. I've been trying really hard recently to deal with it, but I wonder if it's something that is gonna stay with me for life. I hope maybe when I'm with the right person and finally feel safe and secure, it will go away.

When I was in my late teens, I was a size eight and weighed eight stone twelve pounds, and as much as I like my now curvier body, I do look back at pictures of me and love them. I know that's hypocritical after everything

I've said, but I'd be lying if I said I didn't look at the pictures and think I looked good. I could wear almost anything and everything that I wanted and it would look good on me. I didn't have the worries of things being too tight or my legs looking too big, but I was a teenager and my body shape has changed so much since then.

More annoying than anything was that I didn't have to watch what I ate or go to the gym, which is a pet hate of mine. I think anyone who knows me will know that I hate dieting and I hate exercise even more. I was naturally thin and had to put in no effort. I enjoyed the compliments from people, like when I went to Marbella when I was eighteen and everyone kept saying, 'Lauren, you have the best body out of all of us.' It was nice to be complimented, but at that age I took it for granted. I didn't think and obsess about my weight all the time like I do now. I think it's harder to stay slimmer as you get older, and you really have to work at it.

I was nineteen years old when my figure dramatically changed. It was like it happened overnight. Serious. I can remember the exact moment that I caught myself in the mirror as I walked past and had to do a double take. I suddenly had a shape, rather than being straight up and down. I had turned into a woman! My mum and my sisters are all naturally skinny. They don't have a feminine shape like me and they were really jel that I'd suddenly gained some womanly curves. I'm not sure that my new shape had anything to do with the abortion I had around that time. I was very down after that happened, and when I am down, I do comfort-eat, but it wasn't that – it was like my body had matured and I had become a woman. I didn't have a girl's figure any more.

My weight is a constant battle because sometimes I feel really great and then sometimes really crap about myself. As I get older, I seem to get more and more self-conscious and critical. I feel as though I constantly have to try and get over bad comments and bad pictures, day in and day out. It's all anyone seems interested in. It's a lot harder than it's ever been before because people somehow think it's OK to judge me, which really annoys me. I think the reason I am yo-yoing with my weight so much is because all I'm thinking about is what I am eating, when am I training, what I look like. It's a vicious circle and something that I have become more and more fixated on.

When I'm having down moments, I do moan about the way I look. That's mostly after I've seen a picture on the *Daily Mail* online and they are laying into the way I look or dress. I'm like, 'For God's sake, Lauren, lose some weight. You look awful.' It makes me feel crap and I'll try and find clothes that are baggier and cover me up more. Like my arms – I hate my arms. They are flabby and fat and I never want them on show. They need to be halved in size they are so big. Whenever possible I will wear long sleeves to keep them covered. In the summer when I wore a maxi dress, I'd always put a cardigan over the top so that my arms were completely covered.

My legs bother me too. Sometimes I hate them and look at them and think they are huge. I think I might have got them off my dad's side of the family, and in pictures they always look fat. I think maybe if I had skinnier legs, then I could hide the rest of me being a bit bigger. They look really awful and chunky. When I see the pictures of myself, I go red with embarrassment. Then I promise myself that the next time I go out, I will wear something long and cover up my legs. I have always been aware of my weight and wanting to look good, but it's been massively accentuated since I've been in the public eye and nasty comments have made me even more self-aware and critical.

It takes me an age to get ready as it is – everything has to be perfect. I even hate it if my mobile goes off while I'm, say, doing my eye make-up. I need to be calm and relaxed, and I can't stand being rushed – it makes me all panicky. That's become even worse now I know I am likely to get pictured and I am always trying to make sure that the pictures are decent, but sometimes it feels like no matter how hard I try to look good and think I look good, a horrible picture still finds its way into the papers.

It's hard to describe how I feel when people post nasty personal messages about the way I look on websites. I try not to look, but I can't help it – it's kind of addictive somehow. I'll try and stop myself from looking, but in the end I do and then always feel humiliated. I don't know where people get off judging me like that. I only need to be having a bad day and to read a nasty comment for it to send me over the edge. I'm not that close to my family really, so it's not like I call my mum up and chat to her about it like some daughters would, and anyway, I'm too embarrassed to talk about it to anyone. I'm becoming hypersensitive to everything. I know I'm curvy and could do with losing a few pounds, but seriously, are these people for real? Do they realise the damage they could be doing to someone?

Apart from Gemma, I know that I was the biggest girl on *TOWIE*. All the other girls were really slim. Billie is a bit more curvy, and Sam is quite curvy, but they look nice – they look healthy, not too skinny. Sam, I think, fluctuates like me and she'll often cover up. When I was younger, I used to go to Oceana in Marbella and party in belly tops and bikini tops, but there is no way I could do that now, and I know the last time Sam went, she covered up in kaftans, so maybe she feels the same pressure as me.

All the girls from *TOWIE* probably have their own insecurities. I think every girl does in her own way, no matter how perfect her body is. You'll always find something to complain about. I bet even Beyoncé has a part of her body that she hates!

Since I have been in the public eye, the pressure I put on myself to look good is immense. I'm hanging out in places where other celebs are and I find myself looking at them and thinking, I wish my body was like that. I see pictures of Cheryl Cole, Kim Kardashian and Abbey Clancy in the magazines looking good and think, Oh my God, I'm never gonna fit in. Suddenly I'm sharing the front cover of magazines with these people and it makes me feel horrible because I always look the biggest. Every week when the magazines come out, I hope there will be a positive story on me and I won't be splashed across the front looking fat and horrible.

I have never worried as much as I have in the last year about my body. Being single made me really think about my figure, and the thought of starting again in a relationship made me paranoid about how I look. I wanted to be able to wear 'that' little dress when I go out and have a flirt. I don't want to have to hide away my body for ever, for goodness' sake. I am only twenty-six.

I try and dress for my size and wear clothes that I think suit my figure, although I get loads of sh*t for wearing clothes that are too tight – like the dress I wore to the National Television Awards when I looked like Supernanny, or when I wear leggings and I'm accused of 'squeezing' into them. I'm a ten to twelve, which is a size under the national average, so I'm not that big, am I? I just look big when you compare me to some Skinny Minnie size zero. I have to confess that I hate buying clothes that are a size twelve, but I know that buying a size larger can often be so much more flattering. With swimming costumes and bikinis I haven't got an issue with it, but with clothes it's like I have a mental barrier and because of that I have often bought a size below, knowing that a bigger size would have looked a lot better.

Generally, I try and draw attention to the parts of my body that I like, and I don't always follow fashion if it doesn't suit me. Last year, for instance, it was cool to wear those short shorts and boots, but I stayed well away. There was no way I was ever gonna wear something like that. I need to wear heels with short skirts or shorts. Flats cut off my legs and make them look chunky. If I do ever wear anything short, I make sure that I've got plenty of fake tan on, which is slimming.

I have done nearly everything to try and lose weight, but I find it really hard and have to be in the right head space. Diets make me feel depressed and tired, and I always want to eat something sweet because I feel so low. I get this weird panicky feeling when I need to eat something – that's how much I hate diets! Anyone can push me to begin a diet or to try and lose weight, but if I'm not in the right frame of mind, I can't commit to it. At the end of last year, for example, I knew I wanted to lose weight, but I was having too much of a good time to start going on a crazy diet that meant eating super healthy and stopping drinking. For the first time I was enjoying eating out with my mates and going drinking at bars and clubs. If my mind's not in it, there's no point.

That's why *Dancing on Ice* came at the perfect time for me. I started training in October last year and it was hard-core. I'd just left *TOWIE* and was doing thirty hours a week at the beginning because I needed to catch up with the other contestants, who had started training before me. After a couple of weeks that dropped down to ten hours a week, but the amount you have to learn in such a small space of time meant that I was putting in extra time to try and get good at it. I didn't wanna look like a mug in front of the country, so that gave me an extra push to practise. Little by little my body started to tone up. It was such a great feeling, and all without some painful exercise regime. I mean, it was exercise, but it wasn't enforced hell, like boot camp or the gym. It was more tiring than anything else, and while I was training, I tried to be really good with what I was eating too. I kept thinking of all the outfits I was gonna have to wear, so I wanted to be prepared. I made sure I was eating fresh fruit and vegetables and not bingeing on all the usual crap. It helped that I was so knackered because I couldn't go out as much. Training on a hangover is grim!

My trainer, Rob, and dance partner, Michael Zenezini, were really patient with me and it gave me the routine that I needed, because I can be a bit crap at sticking with things. For instance, I once had a personal trainer, Laura. I thought that would work really well for me. She came to the house each time and we would work out together. I assumed Laura coming to me would make me exercise, but even that I struggled with. Laura was amazing and I really got on well with her, but the bottom line is, I hate exercising and found myself making excuses for not doing it. I feel bad about it because she was really helping me and I liked her.

I am a bit lazy when it comes to exercise. I'm always after a quick fix and hate pounding the treadmill. Exercise makes me feel sick, like faint and headachy, and that's why I've never stuck to anything – because I'd rather feel OK than like sh*t. I also feel like my body is getting bigger rather than smaller when I exercise, like I am building muscle rather than toning, and I am so impatient. I want immediate results and that's impossible. When I can't see results, I get bored and think it's not working.

I went to boot camp about a year ago. I was supposed to live in so that they could oversee what I was eating, but I had too much on, so did three hours each morning. I'd then rush off, grab some food because the exercise made me so hungry and by lunchtime feel exhausted. It just didn't work for me. Even cutting out carbs didn't work, because when I had a drink, I'd then go and eat something really unhealthy late at night, which is the worst time.

Before training for *Dancing on Ice* started, I tried all sorts of different diets. First, I tried the Cambridge Weight Plan. It is based on shakes and then a proper dinner, although I did wonder what the point was of the dinner – it was hardly very filling! You can only have white fish, and you're not allowed any fruit. I stuck to it as best I could for about three weeks and lost nine pounds, which I was really pleased with. I didn't finish the programme and kept stopping and starting, so next time maybe I can do even better!

My crazy life doesn't help my battle with weight. When I was in *TOWIE*, for instance, we filmed for hours on end. There was food on offer, but it's not the same as being at home preparing your own meals. The waiting around was really difficult if you were trying to lose weight. It's really easy to graze with all the food around, especially the chocolate, crisps and pizza. The other girls would have one slice, but I'd always have more because I was so hungry. Afterwards I'd feel really guilty about it.

Some days I'd go the other way and wouldn't eat a thing. Then when filming was over, I'd binge on anything and everything because I was so hungry. I can be a bit of a binge eater. I never eat breakfast and will go without food all day; then I'll eat all the wrong things because I'm so hungry later on.

My weight can go up and down drastically from one week to the next. I know that if I don't eat for three days, then straight away I can see the difference and will notice I've dropped a few pounds, but of course when I start eating again, I blow up – especially when I drink alcohol. Although I've spent the past few years worrying about how I look and how much I weigh, I don't actually even own a set of weighing scales, but I know from my clothes that I yo-yo. Starving myself made me feel good for a little while, but you can't live like that for ever. Crash-dieting does the trick for the short term, like the times when I've not eaten for two weeks before a photo shoot so that I look good, but then a month later I'll have put all the weight, and some, back on. When you crash diet like that, your body goes into shock, so when you start eating again, it stores the fat. It's very bad for you.

I was probably the most body-conscious person on *TOWIE*, and for the Series 2 promo I made them shoot my bit six times because I thought I looked fat. My arms looked massive and I begged them to use the one that I looked the skinniest in. I wanted to change my body so badly, but it was like I was incapable of doing anything about it. I find it so hard to be focused and see something through.

When I started the Cambridge Weight Plan, I probably wasn't in the best place to lose weight. My body was a long way from where I wanted it to be, so I felt low anyway and it was at the time when Mark and I were not officially together but were still sneaking around seeing one another and I felt like I was in limbo. I'd snack and I couldn't keep my mind focused on any of the diets I was having a go at. I was getting sick with him not agreeing for us to go public, so I thought I needed to do something for me. That was when I decided to take drastic action and enrol on the Deborah Morgan retreat before having the holiday in Marbella. I was there for four days, and in those four days I had no solid food, just juices. They were disgusting. They had all sorts of organic vegetables in them, and there was one that contained avocado, and I hate avocado. They'd have to tell me that it wasn't in there so I could drink it, but I knew because it was all slimy and curdled and was this thick yuck. It was so gross that I'd gag as it went down. Other ones had things like cucumber, lime, celery, beetroot and red pepper. Honestly, they were vile. I couldn't stop weeing the whole time and was starving hungry, but it worked! I lost nine pounds in four days, which was amazing.

The retreat was really good. I was with my friend Lyndsey and we stayed in this big old farmhouse. It was really basic and there was no telly or anything for us. Instead we had talks every day to try and change our views on food and diet, and they would tell us what we were doing wrong. It definitely made me want to lose weight because the results were incredible. Even though I barely slept because the bed was so uncomfortable, my eyes were wide, and my skin was clear, and the weight dropped off. All the toxins were out of my system and it changed my outlook on everything. There was one guy there who was really overweight and he stayed at the retreat for sixty days and lost stones. It was unbelievable. We'd all be up at 7 a.m. and with no make-up on would walk along the beach. That on its own was really refreshing, and I didn't feel worried because I knew no one could get a picture. The walks were followed by bouncing classes, where you each have a small trampette and work out to music. That lasted an hour, and then from 6 p.m. to 7 p.m. we did trampolining.

I think the hardest thing for me was filling my time when I couldn't eat anything and even a cup of coffee was out of bounds. We were only allowed to drink herbal tea, except for a very special treat, when we could have tea with organic milk, but no sugar. I drank coconut oil every day, which is amazing for your body and strengthens your hair and nails. You can buy it from Holland & Barratt, so it's possible to follow the diet once you leave the retreat too. Two spoonfuls of cider vinegar were given to us each day to burn the fat that was in the juices. None of it is exactly tasty, but the results speak for themselves. Since I've been back, I haven't followed the diet religiously, but I have bought a juicer so I can do it at home. I have to be careful, though, because I'm gonna find it hard to make the juices that I don't like, like the avocado one, but I need to so that I get a balanced diet.

The only problem with me is that I get bored and then rebel and that's when my weight yo-yos. If I'm not careful, it will take over my life and I have to keep telling myself that life is for living. I more than anyone know that the saying 'nothing tastes as good as skinny feels' is true, but being straight up and down isn't attractive. You need a few bits to go in and out and to have a bum. I need to feel like a woman.

Those few days of juicing and exercising did me the world of good and on that holiday for the first time in ages I felt good about myself. There were quite a few pictures taken of me with blokes, which is why Mark sent me text essays, and I got a lot of attention, which really boosted my self-esteem. I would definitely do that retreat again, although I probably put it all back on again while I was partying! It gave me the confidence to wear a swimming costume rather than covering my body like I'd been used to doing. I really liked how I looked in the cut-out bikini with tassels that I wore – cut-out bikinis are very flattering. There were a few negative comments made about how I looked, but generally the comments were much more positive, which was a big relief. Everyone had their say on how much weight they thought I had lost. I don't think anyone got it right, which made me laugh. Honestly, my weight is their obsession.

Just before I started *Dancing on Ice*, I was actually probably at my heaviest. I was out partying a lot and living my lost teenage years! I was drinking and eating out, and the weight that I had lost when I was at the retreat definitely went back on. Weirdly, the press kept saying that I looked like I had lost weight, but I hadn't! I was much slimmer when I got engaged, but at that time I got loads of sh★t for how I looked. I'm sure that people who meet me and see that I'm not nearly as big as they imagined think, Oh God, you're the fat girl who went on a diet! #whatajoke

I want to feel body-confident, and at the moment I'm the closest I have ever come to feeling happy in my own skin. I don't have anyone at home passing comment on how I look, and as the months pass, my confidence is definitely growing. I don't even worry about my weight that much any more.

I'm back on the dating scene now and I hate that blokes will see me like the press do, especially at the moment – I would die if I thought the guy I'm getting to know saw any of these articles. I know the footballers all look at the showbiz websites. I feel so embarrassed that they see awful pictures of me looking fat. It really knocks my confidence when I think about it. No guy wants their girlfriend to be talked about as being fat and I used to worry that it would put men off me. However, these days I am far more confident with how I look and actually I loved wearing all the skimpy sparkly outfits on *Dancing on Ice*. It was nice for the first time to be judged on my skills rather than my weight. When Jason made the infamous walrus comment, I didn't take it to heart and laughed it off. Lots of people thought it was harsh, but that's just Jason.

Out of everything I have done, nothing has been as effective at changing my body shape as *Dancing on Ice*. My body is much more toned now and I'm loving it. I am definitely finding a new confidence, and if my body gets better, I know my self-esteem will rocket too. I just need to keep it up.

Although my weight has yo-yoed over the years, and ideally even now I'd like to be a bit smaller still, I would never go to the lengths that I have done in the past – like starving myself or taking herbal diet pills: they made me feel edgy and shaky. My friend gave me them, but instead of taking a whole one, I'd only take half because they made me feel so strange. I think I need to find my optimal weight and then keep it stable at that, rather than yo-yoing all over the place. The inconsistency is really bad for your body, so now the weight is shifting, I want to try and maintain it healthily.

When I was with Mark, he was very body-conscious and was obsessed with his weight and image, and I suppose a part of that had to rub off on me. Mark has always been really into his body and he made me feel as though I should be obsessed with mine too, so there was pressure from all angles. I felt like I had the media, the Internet trolls and my partner all going on about weight and that made me totally obsessed. I guess I still am, because I'm still going on about it!

I don't want to become one of these calorie-counting bores, but when there is such a big spotlight on me, it's hard not to analyse every picture and comment. What I'd have given to have had one picture of the two of us walking along a beach looking good in the papers, but it never happened. I went through a stage of looking at every newspaper and magazine to see what people were saying. That was definitely unhealthy.

Mark would tell me that he was happy with the way I looked, and he used to get really annoyed if people criticised my weight, which gave me a lot of confidence, but even he made the odd comment that made me question the way I looked. I'll always remember that time he told me out of anger that I looked like I was nineteen stone while we were filming for *TOWIE*. It was my first ever episode and I was having a spray tan at Amy Child's salon. I was nervous because of the filming, but even more nervous that I was being filmed in next to nothing, with my body insecurities. I was just wearing my underwear and Mark was furious that I had stripped off. He was like, 'Why are you taking your clothes off?' He didn't want me to show my body to the world. He said I looked like I was nineteen stone, which was pretty nasty. I made out like I was OK with it, but I was so embarrassed and everyone was taking the piss out of me. It's those kinds of comments that made me feel insecure. It made me nervous to film because I'd worry how I looked on telly. It didn't help that when I watched it back, I looked much bigger than I thought I did.

Then there was the 'Mark' tattoo I had, which looked like I hadn't waxed. It was so humiliating. I'd always try and laugh it off, but it did upset me. Which reminds me – I need to have that tattoo completely removed once and for all. I've had it lasered and it's only faint now, but it needs to go!

Mark's attitude was also confusing because I knew that he really did like my figure. Our sex life was good, and I wasn't shy about my body with him. Mark was always very honest with me and would tell me when he thought I was looking bigger; he'd tell me to lose weight when he thought I needed to. That was our relationship.

In fairness to him, if he thought I looked good, he'd tell me too. I think he loved me for myself because he'd tell me that I was the best-looking girl on the show, but he'd then say, 'You could be the best out of all of them and go the furthest if you had a body like them.' At the time Amy Childs was getting all the work and he would say to me, 'You're so much more beautiful, but it's because of her body that she gets a lot of work.' I could see what he was saying, but it still made me feel sh★t about myself.

I often suspected that deep down Mark would have liked me to have been slimmer, and one day I remember he said he thought we might be a more famous couple if we were both slim, because people like to see good-looking, slim people. Even if he didn't mean it to, at the time it put even more pressure on me to lose weight, but I think he knew I was never gonna become anorexic. It was his way of joking. I always cared what Mark thought of me, but if he gave me grief, I'd banter back. He knows that if he didn't exercise the way he does, he would have a belly and I'd tell him that. He's got a good body, but it's not amazing. I have seen better. If he put a bit of weight on, I actually quite liked it because he didn't get so much attention. It bothered me what Mark said, but if I was gonna lose weight, it would be for me rather than anyone else and he knew that. You have to love yourself first. You are who you are and you should be proud of that. If you're threatened by a boy, he's so not worth it.

When I was on my own I had to start from the beginning and work out what I really wanted, who I was and what would make me happy. For so long I had my thoughts controlled and dominated by other people and for the first time I was in control and even now I have met someone, I still am. I'm sure what's happened to me has made me a better person and I know I'm bound to make more bad decisions in the future but one thing's for sure, I have left all the bad energy behind me. 👍

Losing weight for someone else is not the right thing to do; you have to want it for you or it'll never stay off. I always felt that if I lost weight, I'd be more confident in myself and in the relationship and then I'd be able to have a bit more control. I would worry about what Mark thought of the bad pictures of me on magazine covers and how he felt knowing that I was probably one of the heaviest people on the show. He had an image and he's a good-looking boy, so I imagine he'd get a heap of stick about dating me. I'm sure people tweeted him to say things like, 'Why are you with Lauren? You could do better,' and that can't have been nice for him. I wanted him to be proud of being with me, not embarrassed. I'd worry that the more people said that about me, the more he'd wonder what the hell he was doing with me.

There were times when I thought if I was single, I'd be a lot slimmer because we both liked our food and were always going out for dinner. My mistake was having the same-sized portions as him. I thought it would be easy to eat less if I was on my own, but that doesn't really work out because now I'm single, I am out drinking, which is probably the worst thing for gaining weight. A glass of white wine with the girls is the best, and I don't want to have to stop that. My face really bloats when I drink alcohol, though, and I look like I've got mumps! I try to drink vodka – that's the skinny person's drink because it is much less calorific – but I do enjoy wine with a meal. When it comes down to it, living is more important to me than dieting.

The reality is that I haven't got someone cooking for me every day. I'm a normal girl and just like other people and my diet varies from one day to another. Like I said, I don't eat breakfast, but I'll have a sandwich or a jacket potato for lunch and then a proper dinner. One of my weaknesses is Indian food, and if I have a busy day, then I'll grab a takeaway with some friends in the evening. I think twice about it now that my body is of such public interest, but I used to do it all the time without thinking about it. My life hasn't got a routine, so it's hard to eat well all the time. My body isn't stable, because I'm rushing here, there and everywhere, and so my weight isn't gonna be stable either. Training for *Dancing on Ice* was about the most structure I've had in years, but I'm not sure how I can keep that up. I wish I was one of those people who ran around and it just fell off, but I'm not. I have to continually work for it.

I often ask myself if I'd feel happier being slimmer, but I'm not sure I would. I'd really them to lay off me in the press, but I like going out for a meal. I like to be able to have more than one drink without being paralytic because I haven't eaten anything. I'm a normal girl and I really don't think I want to be skinny skinny. Slim with curves suits me fine. I just want to be able to go out and not cop any flak for how I look. That would be ideal.

I suppose the easiest way of shifting weight is to go and have lipo, but there's no way I want to have surgery. I know I'm not a size-zero skinny, but, seriously, do I look like I need weight-loss surgery? I'm not ruling it out for ever, but right now it's a complete no-no for me. It's the cheat's way to lose weight, isn't it? It might be quick and easy, but it's so lazy! I'd rather do it the natural way. Since I've been in *TOWIE*, I get offered all this stuff for free, like boob jobs, nose jobs, lipo and Botox. It's random. I don't mind natural enhancers, like my permanent make-up on my eyes, eyebrows and lips, but nothing too drastic. I got Essjay Hartshorn, who is a permanent make-up artist, to do it for me. It took about six hours, but I think it's worth it. It hurts a bit, but it's more time-consuming than anything. I like it because I always look like I've got a bit of make-up on. I have had my lips lined a few times and they swell up afterwards, so the press think I have had my lips plumped and had collagen put in, but I haven't. After a few days of applying lip balm every couple of hours, they go down, but they look much more defined. It's not that expensive to have it done and I think it's worth every penny.

I think that having surgery can take away natural prettiness. I feel too young to go down that road yet anyway. I had my nose done when I was younger, but that was only because I had an accident and had to have an op to smooth out the bump on the side. My boobs still look good, so why would I go and get a new pair? I like my boobs and prefer to have them a bit smaller and be able to wear more sophisticated clothes or a low-cut top without showing too much cleavage. If I do want some cleavage, then I can always wear a push-up bra, which works really well. One of my biggest hates is when girls have those really fake-looking boob jobs. Maybe once I've had kids, I'll want to get them done, like one of my friends. She has two children and her boobs have never been very big and it was something she always wanted. She thought about having it done when she was younger because she came into a bit of money when she was eighteen, but she decided to wait and eventually she had them done after she had her kids. She has been going through a divorce, so having them done has made her feel much more confident. It's probably the best boob job I have ever seen and they don't look fake at all. You can get really good fake boobs. They don't have to be the stuck-on ones like so many people go for.

I wouldn't judge others for having surgery – I think it is a personal choice – but I definitely think people should wait until they are older to make the decision because so many insecurities that you have when you are younger disappear with age. Surgery is something you have to live with for life, not to mention all the risks.

I think in the celebrity world surgery has become really normal – celebs have boob jobs or Botox like I would go shopping – but it is a big deal and I know that I am definitely not ready to go under the surgeon's knife just yet! The thought absolutely terrifies me. I'm crap at even having to take medicine and I only do when I really have to. I know loads of celebrities turn to surgery because they want to look good without the hard slog and it's a quick fix, but for me that's the lazy choice. Anyway, if I was gonna do it, I wouldn't tell anyone! I wouldn't be setting up photos with paps – that's well embarrassing and desperate.

I feel really uncomfortable with the idea of surgery because I have a lot of young fans. I know I wake up all the time wishing I was half the size, but I know I can lose weight the healthy way if I put my mind to it. What message would I be sending out if I went and had lipo just because it was free or I started to take slimming pills? I think I am a role model and I would hate any of my young fans to think that it was OK and normal and that I was endorsing it. I'm only twenty-six years old and in a way I find it quite bloody offensive that I get it offered to me so regularly. I guess they must be looking at the same websites as me! The ones where I look twice the size of what I actually am. Even so, I think I get approached weekly with weight-loss ideas or programmes or offers of lipo. I'm telling you, everyone is f*cking obsessed. #theyneedtogetalife

I have good days and bad days like everyone with how I look, and I can be my own worst critic. But as time has gone on I have learnt to embrace my body and curves. Although I still desperately want to be photographed and people to say I look good, rather than, 'Lauren, what were you thinking?' I am nearly in a place where I feel confident in myself no matter what anyone says. I think I have turned a corner and the bullies and haters out there don't get to me any more. I have learned to love myself, because it's what's on the inside that counts.

These days I wake up feeling that something exciting is about to happen. I don't hide myself away, scared to show my face. If I do, everyone has won. Of course, there are days when I'd like to change this or that, but moping won't make any difference. I've been given an opportunity and I'm going to take it with both hands.

My Top Ten Tips on How to Be an Essex Girl

1. Most importantly, make sure you are tanned.

2. Go glam and apply some eyelashes.

3. Ensure your nails are manicured. Chipped nails are cheap.

4. Hair extensions are great for styling and give so much body. If you don't fancy sitting for hours having them put in, wear a clip-in.

5. Glamorous dress code. Make sure you're dressed to impress in an outfit that hugs your curves.

6. Christian Louboutin heels. Get saving!

7. Confidence. Boys love a confident girl who knows what she wants.

8. Don't over-accessorise. One statement piece is often enough, such as a quality watch.

9. Range Rover Evoque. Big love for this – just had to have it!

10. Hair. Make sure you get your rollers in and build some height. Nobody likes flat, lifeless hair.

5

Fake Tan? Check.
Peplum Dress? Check.
Extensions? Check.
It's Time to Make Some Money

I HATE WORKING in an office at a desk. Lol. It's mind-numbingly boring and I am so unbelievably glad that I don't have to any more. When I worked for Orrick, Herrington & Sutcliffe, I hated being stuck behind the desk. It was the first bit of independence I had ever really had away from Mark, but instead of getting my head down and working, I'd be thinking about home time and what I was gonna wear that night. I don't know how people do it day in, day out and I feel so fortunate that I am doing what I love now and it's not a nine-to-five job. ☺

I don't always have good things to say about *The Only Way Is Essex*, but on that front it has opened up so many opportunities for me and I'm trying to take advantage of them all. I really want to make sure that when my 'celebrity' work dries up, I have something to fall back on and that's what I am building up with my business, Lauren's Way, which is becoming more and more successful.

I met Nev Mehmet, my business partner, in the first series of *The Only Way Is Essex*. Nev had an apartment in Wrexham Park that he was trying to rent out. He had a call from one of the production crew for the show asking if they could hire it as a location. He had no idea about the show; he was just told by the letting agent that a reality show wanted to use it and he agreed. I was looking for somewhere to live at the time and so it was set up on the show as one of the apartments I was considering! Nev turned up on the day of filming to see what was going on and we started talking and getting to know one another. He asked me about my hair and where I got my hair extensions done. I kept thinking, Why is this guy so interested in my hair?! I didn't realise at first that he has a background in hairdressing and also does hair extensions. He uses this technology called cold fusion, which means no heat or glue is used, which is much kinder to your hair. The bonds are flat and sit close to the head, so they don't pull on the scalp. Because of that, they don't cause the bald spots that some extensions do. #hairextensionsforever

He did mine a couple of times and they were great. He knew so much about hairdressing and beauty. His dad is a colour technician and has owned their family salon, Cheriee, in North London since 1967, and Nev had a hairdressing shop called Blow in Kent, which he later sold. He now has a salon called Wonderful Hair in East London, so he has loads of knowledge. We got on really well and he started to come to Essex Fashion Week with me and do my hair backstage. Before long we decided that we could make a really successful business together. He had loads of contacts, and there was interest in me because of *TOWIE*, so it seemed a really good opportunity. I had been approached by various companies to be the face of their fake-tan products, but I kept thinking, Why would I want to do that when I could do it myself and have my own products? So many celebrities get paid to be the face of something, but I wanted to be part of the whole process and invest my time and effort into something that was mine, rather than just showing up and smiling to promote another person's product. A fake-tanning company approached me and offered me £40,000, which is a big deal, but I turned it down – it wasn't for me.

It was April 2011 when we started up Lauren's Way and at first it was really hard. I don't think I realised what it takes to start up a business from scratch, and at first there's no money in it – it's just hard work.

Fake-tan mousse and lotion was the first product we launched – the normal one, not the Darker than Dark that is now part of the range. It took a long time to get a really good product manufactured and I was involved every step of the way, right from the smell of the tan to the colour to the packaging. I wanted it to be perfect.

Nev used his contacts to source the actual tan. I then went to the factory in North London to look at the products. It was really interesting because I got to go into the labs and test the different products. I smelled them all and could feel the texture of each of the creams and mousses. Then they made me up samples so I could try them out myself and see if they were spot on. The smell of the tan, in particular, was really important to me because I think so many people are put off using it because of that, so I had a few samples made up until I was completely happy that it smelled fresh and not like biscuits. Lol. That's one of the things most commented on – that Lauren's Way tan smells good.

I also had to be sure that the colour was good and didn't streak or fade too quickly. Because I use fake tan all the time and am a massive fan, I was very clear on what I did and didn't want. It was only when I was really happy with everything that I gave it the thumbs-up.

Next I had to work out what the packaging for the tan would look like. We had a graphic designer show us examples of the labels. I wanted something simple and sophisticated. Finally we were shown the prototype of the range. It took about three months from start to sign-off, but it was a steep learning curve for me and I really enjoyed it. I think it's probably the most focused thing I have done, but I learned so much and couldn't believe how much I liked being involved in something like that. As I said earlier, I'm not very good at sticking to things that I don't like – I never have been – but to produce my own products from start to finish was really satisfying.

The start-up costs were high, so to keep them down, we began by advertising the tan on Facebook. The response was amazing! There was a massive market for it and we could barely keep up with demand. Advertising it via Facebook meant that we had time to set up a website, and it gave us a good indication of how well it would be received by the public.

At that stage just a few of us were working for Lauren's Way, mainly people Nev or I knew, so that we could trust them with what was going on. Now we employ twenty-six people. Nev and I just haven't got time these days to interview people – we have an office and shop manager who does that for us – but I get on with everyone who works for me and a lot of them have become really good friends of mine – like Lauren Meyler, who is a make-up artist and does hairstyling two days a week. She stays at my house all the time and we are always going out to bars and clubs together. It's like a big family in a way, and I'm really proud of how far we have come in the space of a year and a half.

When we knew that the mousse and lotion were selling well, we sat down and came up with more products to extend the range, including Glam Tan for nights out on the town, tanning mousses for a lasting tan, but also an instant bronzed glow, a gradual tan and a wash-off tan, plus all the tanning accessories, like body polishes and mitts. We even do fake tan for men. I've got it all covered! Recently I launched the Darker than Dark range, which with one application does make you darker than dark! #ilovebeingbrown

They have all been so successful with customers, and on the website (laurensway.com) you can read customers' reviews of each of the products, which give a really good idea of how user-friendly the products are. I think they have definitely sent a shockwave through the tanning and beauty industry. Companies seem surprised at how well Lauren's Way has done in such a short space of time and without a huge amount of money to market and promote it. If you look at companies like St Tropez who are massive, they never achieved what we have achieved in a year. What we've done is pretty amazing and I am so proud. The company is also a part of the Made in Britain campaign, so all my products are made in the UK, which is really appealing to people, I think.

Social networking sites like Twitter and Facebook have played a massive part in the company's success, and people are always tweeting the salon or me to tell me how much they love the products, which is great instant feedback. This is gonna sound weird, but I get so much sh*t over my weight or the way I dress or Mark that it feels great to have something that no one gets at me about. It's the one thing that they can't seem to find a flaw with and that people seem to love. I don't get criticised for it, just a lot of love, and that gives me some much-needed confidence.

Because the tans were going so well, we decided to grow the business further still. We were having such strong, positive feedback that we thought it would be a good time to extend the range. We didn't want to dilute the tanning range, because that is how the business started and what it's known for, but we wanted to try and provide something that no one else did. I wanted to give people the opportunity to get the complete

Essex look, so we started doing lashes that anyone can use. They are so easy to apply, but they are dramatic and glamorous and suit everyone. I also launched Dream Rollers, which have been really successful. You put them in before you go to bed and then they do the work while you are asleep. The rollers flatten when you rest your head on them and are key in getting that Essex look. And finally we now sell clip-in hair extensions, which are really good.

I can remember buying a Jessica Simpson hairpiece when I was younger because I loved her, but when I got home and put it in, it looked rubbish! I sold it for a tenner at a boot sale to an African woman. It made me realise that I didn't want people to buy something just because they might like me. I wanted people to buy it and love it because it's a really useful product. I made sure that they were tried and tested so that they would look good on anyone. And we've won an award too! We got presented with 'Best Cosmetics Brand' at the National Luxury and Lifestyle Awards in aid of the charity War Child. The awards celebrate top luxury brands and influential personalities, so that was a real honour for me and really put us on the map. We are still growing, but already Lauren's Way offers customers the opportunity to get that Essex look and is going down a storm.

On holiday in
Las Vegas

Mark being
cheeky poolside

A night out on the town with my Essex girls

Papped!

My glam squad work their magic

The publicity shot for the third series of *The Only Way Is Essex*

At the *Twilight* premiere with Lauren Pope

Ready to paint the town red with Lydia and Arg

Stealing a kiss
on a gondola in
romantic Venice

The show captured all of the highs and lows of my relationship with Mark

Confiding in Lydia

Mark in his element

I love to get glammed up for a night out

On a night out with my Lauren's Way girls – we have become good friends

WEARING
EXOTIC SKINS KILLS

- Leave Wildlife out of Your Wardrobe -

LAUREN GOODGER for **PeTA**

Animals have always had
a special place in my heart
so I was chuffed when
PETA asked me to help
with their campaign

Bracing myself for
a charity walk

The grand opening of my first salon Lauren's Way

Caught out with my rollers in!

The salon opening with Chloe Sims and Frankie Essex

Independent woman!
Supporting a cause
close to my heart

Jazz hands. Getting
ready to hit the ice

That's the concept behind my salon too – creating the Essex look, but in true celebrity style. I opened it in February last year. It used to be Chantelle Houghton's salon and we took over the lease when she decided to close her boutique because she was having a baby. I sublet it off her, but there were problems straight away and it really made me think about whether it was something I should be doing. We'd only be in there a week and I was just getting everything set up when the shop was egged. It was horrible, because I was thinking, Who would do this to me? What have I done to you?

It felt really personal, and I'm such a fearful person that it made me want to call it all off and forget about the whole thing. I was terrified that somebody was out to get me and any progress or confidence that I had vanished. It only got worse, because the night before we had external shutters fitted, the shop was petrol-bombed. I was in the cinema when I got the call from Nev to tell me. I'll never forget it. My body went kind of numb. You know when your heart races and you feel sick? It was like everything was going on around me, but I wasn't a part of it. I felt panicky and didn't wanna believe what I was hearing. It was bad enough having the shop egged, but to have someone come and petrol-bomb it was something else. I was at the cinema with Lisa and was in such a blind panic that I got up, looked at her, said, 'The shop is on fire,' ran out of the cinema and left her there! I didn't even know what I was doing.

I rang Mark while I was in the car on the way to the shop. He was the first person I called and he told me straight away not to have it filmed for the show. He said the same thing had happened to his club and not to worry about it. He said he thought it would look tacky if they did film it, but I was like, 'My shop is burning down. The last thing I'm thinking about is whether they are gonna film it.' I was in a blind panic and kept thinking, Imagine if someone had been in there.

When I got to the shop, it was like a scene from a disaster movie. There were fire engines and police and loads of people standing around looking at what was going on. Frankie Essex and her friend came down to see if I was OK, but I wasn't. I was really shaken up. There was a guy there who had chased the boy who'd done it. Bless him. He was a friend of Argent's family and I'd never even met him before. He was really brave because the boy had a crowbar and had smashed this guy's car up with it as he ran away.

I was so frightened. Who hated me that much that they would do something like that? Was it because they wanted me to fail, or was it a random act? At the time it made me feel really scared. It really shook me up.

Even now, nearly a year on, no one has been caught, and no one knows why they did it, which makes me feel a bit edgy in itself. The thought that there are people out there happy to do something like that is creepy.

Fortunately, the damage wasn't as bad as it could have been, or as bad as it looked when I first turned up. The internal shutters had stopped the fire from spreading too far into the shop. The bomb had smashed the front of the shop and burned all the wood, though. Thousands of pounds' worth of products were ruined because the heat from the fire had bent and melted the plastic bottles, and all the chairs and displays were wrecked. It was a huge setback for us. Not only had it cost a heap of cash, but it also meant that we couldn't open for another week or so.

We had a team of people working round the clock on the shop and they did an amazing job. I felt really deflated and angry that it had happened, and if I hadn't had the right people around me, it might have stopped me in my tracks. In the end though it made me stronger, and realise that I shouldn't let the bullies get the better of me.

Once we got the shop back up and running, I made sure that the security was really sorted out. Now there's CCTV, so if it were to happen again, we should be able to catch the little bastards. I hope to God it doesn't. There was obviously a lot of attention from the press over my shop and I was asked to go on *Daybreak* to talk about it. Randomly, they'd also heard that I was Kate Middleton's favourite character from *TOWIE*! So weird, but I was like, 'Yeah, that's cool.' I can't imagine her and Will sitting down and watching us. It's just such a strange, strange thought, but I love the idea. Kate is naturally really beautiful, and so stylish and sophisticated. I wonder if she'd like some of my Lauren's Way fake tan or lashes?!

The vandalism to the shop so early on was a real blow to the business, to my confidence and also to the people in the area. It scared a lot of locals because the salon is on a really nice, quiet road in Buckhurst Hill, and people round that way weren't used to things like that happening. That put even more pressure on me because I thought that the locals might resent me for having the boutique and bringing lots of people from outside the area in. I do think a lot of them aren't very keen on the concept of the salon, which is to give you the Essex look, and Nev reckons that some people in Essex don't think the cast of *The Only Way Is Essex* represent Essex in the right way and give it a bad name. I suppose some people probably feel like that, but we do have a lot of locals book into the salon. They mainly come in during the week, as over the weekend it is filled with tourists and fans. We do big business on the weekends and it can be crazy in there.

I try and go down as much as possible, and I always go in to get my hair done, about three times a week. When I do, I make sure that I spend time with people and speak to them. So many of them have travelled for miles to see me, which is an amazing feeling and I owe it to them to spend that time having my picture taken and chatting with them. The salon has been so popular and such a success we are looking at franchising it across the country. I can't believe that we have achieved so much in a year. I have to pinch myself to think that my shops could be laid out across the UK. Lauren's Way could be nationwide. It's amazing. Lol.

Seven months after we launched the business, we started to get interest from the beauty and hairdressing trade. Nev tells me that will give the company real longevity, which is exactly what we want. The trade side of the company is very important because it means that salons all over the country can stock and use Lauren's Way products. So you won't have to come to my salon or just go on the Internet to buy them – customers will be able to get them in their local salon. The products will be in the hands of professionals, which will give the person buying the stuff trust in the products, which is so important for me and the company to continue doing well.

Last October Debenhams started to stock Lauren's Way products in all of their flagship stores, which is incredible. I went to launch it in their Dublin branch and have been to various different stores to promote it. It's doing really well and our Christmas packages were a big hit. We put together gift sets that had lashes in, tan, a mitt, moisturiser – the whole Essex look – and they were very popular.

We've also had interest from Amazon and Argos. My dream would be to have Lauren's Way in Boots and Superdrug – because that is the exact market I think my products appeal to – but we'll have to wait and see.

I'm not even a year and a half into this and we've already done way better than I thought possible. They say that with a new business you don't make a profit for a long time, but we've already started to take money out and are able to pay ourselves, which is a big thing. Sorry, I'm making it sound like it's really easy, but it's not. We do a lot of work behind the scenes and I travel all over doing trade shows where we showcase everything and people can buy some of the products to see what they are like. At the Professional Beauty Show in Manchester last October, Lauren's Way had a stand and I went up there to promote it. We took a vanload of products up with us, but after one day we had completely sold out! We had to get someone to drive another van up for the Sunday. It was mental. #manchesterloveslaurensway

I am always trying to think of new ideas that could work and be a success, so Nev and I have meetings all the time. We have just started our latest venture – Essex Angels. Basically, if you can't get to my salon, we'll come to you! Our Essex Angels will get you looking a million dollars before your big night out. I'm hoping it will really take off.

I think what I've learned, and I've learned a hell of a lot, is that you have to have a team of professionals around you for anything to work well and be a success. I know that I need to become more savvy, and there are areas I'm still learning about and exploring, but the bottom line is, I want this company to be in a position where if I'm not famous tomorrow, it can still thrive. I think we're just about there. I'm even getting interest from Australia and America in stocking my products, which is unbelievable. To have Lauren's Way products stocked in other countries is a dream, and I'm gonna try and make it a reality. Although I have got a long way to go, that is something to shout about. That is a big achievement and I am beyond proud. ☺

Lauren's Way has been a big part of my working life,

but I have done loads of other stuff too. In fact, my feet have barely touched the ground in the last couple of years. I have been a busy girl! When I was taken on by Max Clifford Associates in June 2011, I knew I had the best people around me to help me sort out my life! Max has got great contacts and I have been so lucky with all the things I have been involved in.

A lot of the guys from *The Only Way Is Essex* make their money from personal appearances. You can make quite a bit of cash from it – like £2,500, at least, a night – but I have stayed away from doing that. I did a few at the beginning, but not anymore. I'm really lucky that I've got so many other bits and pieces going on that I haven't had to do them lately.

Obviously Lauren's Way has had a massive pull on my time because it's a growing business in its early stages, but also I've got involved in a load of other things. I've even had my own jewellery range launched, which was wicked. It was last September and I was approached by Lisa Sanders, who is a jewellery designer and owns Hot Rocks. She's designed for loads of celebrities before – like JLS, Lady Gaga and the Saturdays – so I thought it would be really cool to do something with her. I did it under the Lauren's Way banner, so it was us kind of teaming up together. As I said earlier, I'm not the biggest fan of jewellery and I really only like statement pieces. My pet hate is when people where a load of jewellery, as it detracts completely from what they are wearing. Like, if I was wearing earrings, I wouldn't wear any other jewellery. So I wanted to design something that I would like to wear and that represented my fashion ideas. I love being part of things like this and I can't believe that I am. It's the stuff of dreams really.

I was involved in the whole process. I think if you're gonna put your name to something, then you have to believe in it. We had a few meetings at Max's office and I got to design my very own range. Lauren's Way has a heart in its logo, so hearts feature heavily. The range is girly and I think good for the young market. I love the bracelet with the heart charm, and I wear the white watch with diamantés all the time. It's not an expensive range, so it's accessible to everyone, but it's blingy and glamorous, not chavvy. During the process I got shown various prototypes and the bits I didn't like were changed. On one of the pieces, for example, the gem was too big, so I had it made smaller. The key is whether I would wear it myself, and if the answer is yes, then it's a goer. All the jewellery that I helped design is very chunky and statement because that's what we wear where I'm from and I wanted it to have that Essex feel. I'd like to do more collaborations like this, but perhaps a make-up range or my own nail varnishes so I can concentrate on beauty.

I did start my own clothing range. I'm lucky because I get to meet quite a few people in the industry who link me up and I was offered the chance to design and create a range. As always I spent a lot of time making sure the outfits were what I would wear. I did some drawings myself and a designer made them more professional! I went to look at loads of different fabrics and again spent ages choosing what I'd like, like stretchy materials. When they were made up, though, they were nothing like what I'd imagined. They have been selling them under Lauren's Way in New Look, and I am a bit embarrassed to say that I'm not sure I like the finished product as much as the designs. There was a catwalk show at One Marylebone in London to display the different pieces – there were eleven different styles – and they sold very well online. If I did something like this again I think I'd like to be more involved as I don't think I devoted as much time as I should have.

I'd like to revisit doing a clothing line in the future, but right now I need to focus on the beauty side of things. Once I have that sorted maybe I can look again at doing clothing. Next time, though, I would want to make sure that it is as I designed it. I can't ask people to buy something that I wouldn't wear, can I?

How to Start a Business in Ten Easy Steps

1. Find a good product and do your research.

2. Establish who your competition is.

3. Find a company and social media name that no one else can get their hands on.

4. Price into the market place.

5. Research how you will sell your product.

6. Plan everything, even what you're gonna wear to a meeting.

7. Make sure your product looks good. Looking good is important.

8. Set your sights on the high-street retailers.

9. Get good people working for you.

10. Make sure that wherever you set up is in a cool location that'll get noticed.

I get approached to do a lot of things and I can't do everything, so it's my management who advise me on what would be good for my career and what would kill it on the spot! They set up the meetings and I turn up! That's basically how it works, which is good because I'm not very organised and need to be told what to do half the time!

Not so long ago I was asked to be the face of a new online dating site. I suppose that I have an 'unlucky in love' reputation, but straight away I was like, 'No way! How dare they ask me to do that! Do they think I need to go online to find someone?' I really didn't like the idea. Fair enough if people who don't like going out wanna do it, but I like to socialise and I haven't got a problem speaking to boys. To me, it sounded a bit desperate and the suggestion that I had to go online to get a bloke I didn't like at all! I'm a young girl. Why would I want to be the face of something like that? I'd only just properly split with Mark and there was no way I was gonna consider doing it. Even if I was twenty years older and single, I don't think I'd want to meet guys on a dating website. I'd worry what they might be like when you got to meet them. They might be awful! I have to believe in something to be a part of it and so I turned it down – that's just the way I am. I'm happy to say that online dating isn't for me. I kept thinking what Mark would think if I did it and he'd probably piss himself laughing. I'm not body-confident. The world knows that now, but when I got asked by a theme park to promote a new ride, I thought it sounded like fun. That was until they told me that they wanted me to dress in a *Baywatch* swimsuit. Can you imagine me doing that? Seriously, I can't think of anything worse and all I can imagine is the grief I'd get from the press over how I looked in the costume. It would have properly stressed me out and I'd have had panic attacks in the days leading up to it. The idea of people generally scrutinising my body makes me wanna vom. No way. I'll decide who sees my body, thank you very much. I'd have been setting myself up to look like a bloody mug. That one didn't need to be thought about very hard at all before I said no. It's well tacky when I think about it. Thank God I turned it down!

Being in this business has given me so many amazing opportunities and I know I am really lucky, so I always wanna give something back and try and get involved in as many charity things and campaigns as possible.

Last April PETA (People for the Ethical Treatment of Animals) approached me to see if I would front a campaign for them. Hilariously they wanted me because I was the *TOWIE* member that they had received least complaints about! I knew that PETA did loads of work with really high-profile celebrities like Pamela Anderson, Eva Mendes and Simon Cowell, so I was really interested in what they wanted me to do. When they told me, though, I was proper freaked out. I was taking such a battering in the press about my weight and here they were asking me to pose naked for them. #ohsh*t! I really wanted to do it, but I felt so low about how I looked. The constant scrutiny I was under made me nervous so I had to really think about it. At the same time I knew that it was a good thing to do and was for a great cause. They wanted to paint me to look like a snake to highlight the cruelty of exotic skins for fashion. I was shown some really awful footage of animal cruelty and I thought, I've just gotta do this. I can't think about me. If I can make a difference, then I've gotta do it. I think most people think of cute, cuddly animals suffering, but to see what I saw made me realise that any cruelty to animals has to be stopped. It was sick.

I arrived at a studio in London and basically had to get my kit off! It was a bit awkward because there was a male photographer and assistant there. I had to position myself on this block and it was quite uncomfortable. I tried to hide my bits so the blokes couldn't see the whole time, and it was so bloody cold that they had to put two heaters on! It took eight hours to hand-paint my body, but it was incredible and the final image was unveiled in Covent Garden. I couldn't believe it when the campaign received the biggest press response they had ever seen in the UK. It was the first time in history that one of the UK-based celeb campaigns had been covered by a national TV news channel. I thought the pictures were really cool and hardly had to be touched up at all, which made me feel good about myself. I'd definitely like to do it again if they wanted me back.

It's shoots like the PETA one that I really love because they are different but cool and worthwhile. I've done a heap of stuff that I hate for various magazines, but that's part of the job. You have to take the rough with the smooth, I suppose. The one thing I do hate is when I'm made to look like someone else and can barely recognise myself. After a couple of shoots in *OK!* I've looked at the pictures and wondered who that person is. I don't know what they do to my face!

I'm also really fussy about my make-up and how it's done, so when I go on shoots and hate the make-up, I go to the toilet and add some. I feel a bit embarrassed about doing that, but I can't bear the idea of being pictured not looking my best.

I loved the *More* magazine one that I did because it was really fun. Mostly, because it wasn't focused on my body! Quite often the shoots I do are because everyone is obsessed by it, so there are a lot that I'm not keen on and in which I have to show parts of my body that I hate. I'd rather do something else, but that's where the interest is and I get that, so I always end up having to talk about it.

My dream one day would be to feature in *Vogue*. That would be amazing. I love the high fashion magazines in which they make you look really cool and beautiful rather than cheesy. I could have a different look and the high cheekbones and be really striking! I would love that. They could make me look like a model! #yesplease

I've obviously just done *Dancing on Ice*, which was amazing, but I'd like to do more TV work if I can. I don't wanna try and be a presenter or anything – everyone seems to do that – but I've got a couple of pipe dreams. You are gonna think I'm mad, but I would *love* to have an R&B single. Just one video in which I look amazing – that would be so cool. I wanna be like J Lo. I love her. Simon, are you reading this?! We are under the same management! Lol. And if I can't have that, I'd like to be on *The X Factor* panel, please. Ooh, I'd love to be a judge! Lol.

Last year I was asked to do something A. Mazing. I absolutely *love* Kim Kardashian. I love everything about her! The people who run her website, Shoe Dazzle, approached me to see if I'd be interested in designing a shoe for the UK launch of the website. Oh. My. God. I was so excited. There was no way I was gonna say no. I am so annoyed, though, because the company have decided to postpone their UK launch. I'm gutted, to be honest, because I would love to work with Kim. I really hope that they get some funding and it happens.

I have never met Kim, but it's something I really want to make happen. I knew she was at Movida one night and I could have gone down, but it felt a bit sad, like a crazed fan trying to speak to her. I am supposed to be doing her boot camp in Los Angeles soon, so maybe I'll meet her then. That would be ace. To me, she has the best body. She's not stick-thin – she's got a big bum and she's proud of it. She stands up for all the curvies and I love her for that. She seems to have a really fun personality, and what I like about her is that she hasn't forgotten her roots – you don't see her trying to become a TV presenter, do you? She came from reality TV and she's proud of it. I also love her fashion and make-up. She has the best make-up artist with her. He contours her face and shades it so it looks very chiselled. It's wicked. I'm gonna get back on to them to see if anything has changed because I would love to work with her. I'm running away with myself, but how amazing would it be to have a clothing line with her or to do a make-up range together?

I feel so privileged to be able to have these opportunities, but I wanna be able to give something back too. I have got involved in a few charities – in particular, Jo's Trust. I was really interested because it's the only cervical cancer charity in the UK, and because I have had issues and so have members of my family, I thought it would be something I could help with. The charity promotes being vigilant about symptoms and campaigning for people to attend screening appointments. I took part in their 5K Walk for Life in Hyde Park last June, and I'm hoping to do it again this year. It's weird the kind of power that Twitter has because when I started to tweet about what I was doing, Jo's Trust Twitter followers went up by twenty per cent. That's wicked. I can't believe that I have the power to do that, but I'm so pleased because it makes all the difference.

I don't have a close-knit family, but I hope that when I get married and have children, I will have a close family around me. I hate the idea that there are old people who have no one at Christmas, so I participated in a campaign the *Sun* did in 2011, to try and encourage readers to spend time with an elderly person who would be alone over the festive period. I went and visited an old lady in her home for a cup of tea and chat. When I arrived, I was introduced to Margie. She was so sweet. I'm sure she had no idea who I was, and I bet she had never watched *The Only Way Is Essex*, but I liked her even more for that. It didn't matter who I was because all Margie wanted was some company and I could give her that. It felt very fulfilling. She had no one, yet she was bubbly and happy and I really enjoyed chatting to her. We sat together in the communal area talking for ages. Margie told me that she goes to the local café whenever she can, but sometimes her legs are too bad to walk there, which made me feel so sad. There was no sadness from Margie, though. She was so positive and saw the bright side of everything.

I found it hard to see her all on her own, especially at Christmas, and it made me grateful for the people I do have around me who love me. People who have got families around them are so lucky and should never take them for granted.

Because I get looked after by Max Clifford, he has a lot of high-profile clients like Simon Cowell, so I get to go to events that he is hosting, which is pretty cool. Last February I went to afternoon tea at the Dorchester, which was hosted by Simon and Max in aid of the children's hospice Shooting Star Chase. I'd met Simon before, when I entered *The X Factor* in 2004. I hadn't properly spoken to him back then, so when I did, I was surprised at how different he was to the way I thought. The thing that I really couldn't believe was that he actually recognised me! I was like, No way. Is this for real?

He came over to me and shook my hand and said, 'How are you doing?' We had a bit of a chat and I really couldn't believe that he even knew who I was. I was a bit star-struck! I wanted to ask him if I could have my picture taken with him, but I didn't think that would be a very cool thing to do. Luckily, the press wanted pictures and we posed together, so I got the picture! There were a load of celebrities there, like McFly and Louis Walsh, but I sat next to Simon's mum for the tea and she was lovely. It was quite weird having afternoon tea with a load of celebs and *the* Simon Cowell's mum! It's times like that when I think about what I was doing a few years ago. I'm very privileged. I spent the afternoon talking to some sick kids who are being helped by the charity. Things like that really put your life into perspective. I wanna help that charity as much as I can. I love kids and they are all so brave.

I have been a part of and achieved so much in the last couple of years and I feel so lucky. I will never take it for granted and I will continue to be grateful as I grow my business and try new business ventures. If it all ends tomorrow, I know that I'm set up for life and that is an amazing feeling. ☺

My Top Ten Business Tips

1. It's so important to have a good team of people around you.

2. You need a product that works and that you know will sell. Once you've got that, then add the marketing and PR. Take each step at a time and focus on one thing.

3. Have fun and enjoy it. I don't always love travelling and doing all the interviews and exhibitions, but you have to take the good with the bad. I have fun with my team and we have a laugh. When it's not fun, we crack jokes and make ourselves have fun! I have faced so many hurdles for as long as I can remember with everything in my life, but

I've worked hard and have always tried to laugh. I am a happy person and that attracts people to me. If you are a decent person, then friends and colleagues want to be there for you through the hard times and want to share in your success.

4. Be positive and committed. Believe in yourself. If I can, anyone can.

5. Be a good person. Someone can be beautiful and have a horrible attitude and that negative energy pushes people and everything positive away. It's about what's on the inside too.

6. I can talk to anyone – any age, any colour, any race or belief – and get along with them. I am always warm, but not overly confident. I am a nervous person, and believe it or not, I get shy. I'm a normal girl and will stay normal.

7. Things will always get in the way. Mostly life will get in the way, and if you're like me, the odd party. It's those hurdles, those days you have to get up and work when you are totally hanging that make you and the product a success.

8. Don't sit back – always look forward and be proactive. Never stop looking for something better.

9. Have a strong brand image. I did a lot of research with mine and it paid off.

10. Don't give up! Follow your dreams because anyone can do what they want to do if they put their mind to it. I am living proof of that.

6

There Are Celeb Friends and
Then There Are Real Friends

MOODY, JEALOUS, CONFRONTATIONAL, controlling, desperate and weak – that's how I think I came across on *The Only Way Is Essex* and that makes me really sad. My true friends don't think that's the real me. That's the thing with TV – most people are seen as characters so the storylines make sense, and I feel that mine was all too often seen as bitchy and mad. I'm not gonna lie – I have a lot to thank the show for, and I wouldn't be where I am now if I hadn't been given that opportunity, but I feel I was often made out to be in the wrong, always like the nutter and always like a mug. It got to me. I worried that that's what the public thought of me. As a result, I'm forever trying to prove that I'm a better person than that, which is tiring and an uphill battle. I don't know if I can ever change people's opinions, but I'm hoping my side of the story will shed some light on what really went on, not just the edit that people saw.

I was never gonna win with Mark around. It's probably because he's a real charmer. Mark once told me last year – with a deadpan face – that he was dating a member of Girls Aloud. He said it without a hint that he might have been joking. At first I was like, 'No way,' but he kept on and told me that they had to be careful because of the press finding out. He really made me believe him, and it wasn't until a couple of months later that he told me he had made it up. I can't believe I fell for it – cringe! Mark had that knack – he made me and everyone around him hang on his every word. I couldn't understand why he had such a hold over people.

Although I'm grateful for the opportunity, filming *TOWIE* was not an altogether happy chapter for me. In the end I paid a high price and I was unhappy at how I came across. I'm not sure how viewers see it and how much they think is real, but a lot of it is about making a scene and a drama – like when I pushed Mark into the pool at Kirk's house in the first series. The producers must have known that Mark didn't like me going out, so it was a good opportunity to let viewers see for themselves. I was waiting in the car for hours for Mark, wondering what he was getting up to, so when I finally got let out and could go in, I went mad and chucked him in the pool. It was probably very entertaining for viewers. At first the show seemed fun and a bit of a laugh, but as time passed, it became less and less enjoyable. I'd find it annoying knowing stuff but thinking the public were seeing something different. I always wanted them to see the full picture, which they never did.

I totally got that it was a reality TV show, and that some situations needed to be arranged. If this wasn't done then it wouldn't make good television, but when it's your life being affected, it can get really bloody annoying. I'll never forget the time that Lydia split up with Argent. She was crying and I was crying with her; it was such an emotional scene. I knew what breaking up with someone on TV felt like and I wanted to be there for her. The producers even clapped at the end because we had got so emotional and they thought it was gonna make great TV. For once I was being shown in a decent light and was happy that my caring side would be given some airtime, but they never showed it. I couldn't f*cking believe it.

I phoned the producers straight away and asked them why they had done that. They had said at the time that it was really good and emotional, yet they had cut it out and instead shown a bit of me where I looked like I couldn't give a damn about Lydia and Argent. I was so pissed off. I was told that we had given too much away while we chatted and they needed to save that for later in the series. It made me feel like no matter what I did, they would always have the power to edit the footage. I felt like I gave up at that point. I had the proper hump about it, but it wasn't going to change. That was the bottom line. The viewers liked drama, and the drama mostly came from me. But I looked like I had the hump all the time and was moody and miserable, they got what they wanted, but they were never letting me be me. Where's the drama now? There isn't any.

As I said earlier in this book, the impact the show had on Mark and my relationship was catastrophic really. Yes, there were massive problems between us before the show started, but once it was under public scrutiny and I could see what he was up to, it all started to fall apart at the seams. I suppose I could think it did me a favour and showed me what he was really about, but it also made me look like a mug for putting up with so much sh*t. Behind closed doors I could forgive him and we could work it out, but it wasn't so easy when everyone knew what he'd done. I was always so weak, in a way I still am, with Mark and he was always able to get round me and talk his way out of situations, but with everyone watching I felt like I couldn't just forgive him and move on from it because people would judge me for being so soft. That put loads of pressure on me and us as a couple. Rightly or wrongly, that was hard to deal with.

I know I'm not perfect – far from it – but no matter what Mark had done wrong or how bad it was, I still feel like it was me who came off worse. I felt people watching at home would think, Well, he's cheated, but I can see why – she's such a bitch. One time I read a comment saying, 'Mark Wright had a lucky escape. Who would want this as a wife?' I hated that because when the cameras were off, we were a genuine couple. We weren't fake for the show – we were the only real bit half the time – so it hurt all the more.

It felt like because our relationship was genuine but stormy and made good TV, we were really taken advantage of. I don't think anyone ever stopped to think how either of us felt. I think they just assumed that we wanted to be famous and would go along with anything to achieve that. Mark may have been like that, but I wasn't. The time they set up the kiss between Mark and Sam and made me catch them is a classic example. I don't think they will ever know how much that hurt me or how much I cried when I got home that night. Gradually those situations began to irritate me and make me want to walk away.

Even the people on the show were changing. The situation made them so competitive and jealous of one another and they started to do anything to try and get themselves a storyline and airtime. It was pathetic and ridiculous, and I didn't want to be around it any more. The pressure about the way I looked also affected my decision to leave. As I've said before, I felt enormous when I was being filmed next to the other girls on *TOWIE*. I'd beg the producers not to show my legs and hide them under tables so that I'd get less flak from the Internet bullies, but it was no good and I still copped it. So me quitting was a long time coming and had been on my mind for a while before I did it, but I was determined to do it on my terms and when I wanted. It could have been a lot sooner − like when I was suspended in May last year when I had a row with one of the producers. Talking about it makes me annoyed because they were so out of order, but I want to set the record straight.

I had been called to film and had been in a room waiting for hours. I'd recently fallen out with Jess, Mark's sister, and her family were all in there too. It was really uncomfortable and awkward for me. It was so stressful and I was starving. I hadn't told anyone, but I was on the Cambridge Weight Plan as I was trying to lose weight. I didn't have my sachets with me so I had to break my diet by eating regular food, which really pissed me off. We were all moaning about how long they were keeping us hanging around in this room and then, at 1.30 a.m., they told us we wouldn't be needed. I was so furious after waiting for so long and the red mist came down. It was such a waste of my time. It was ridiculous. I kept asking them why they had kept us for so many hours and then changed their minds, but there weren't any answers. I was shattered and drained and it pushed me over the edge. I told them to stick the show up their arses, that it was a load of sh*t anyway. I shouted and screamed and was quite rude to them, which I regret now, but I was fuming about it. I told them how unprofessional they were and was like, 'You're a joke.' The result was, I got suspended from the show for three weeks, which was pretty much the whole series. I didn't get on very well with that producer, although we have since put it behind us. I think she wanted to show her authority and didn't like me telling her what I thought, so she suspended me. I'm not the first person who has been suspended by her, but it was me who got all the press attention. Several of the cast were called in about their behaviour and future in the show and got into trouble, but it was all kept quiet.

With another producer, Mike, it was a different story. I became really close to him. In fact when he was producing, it could cause a bit of tension because other cast members thought I was the favourite, although it didn't feel that way most of the time! He saw me through the fun times, like when we were fighting paps off with an umbrella at my engagement party. He used to throw me in the car and hide me when he didn't want me to be papped because of storylines. We used to have a real laugh about it all and I think he understood how much it got to me at times. He has seen me at some of my lowest points and would always be there if it got too much.

Anyway, the time I got suspended, I hold my hands up – I did go mad and say things I probably shouldn't have, and for that I apologise, and did apologise to them at the time, but the way they treated me by the end pushed me to my limit and I wasn't prepared to put up with it. I lost my head. #everyonehasthosemoments

I can't knock it completely – that wouldn't be fair, and I know without it I'd probably still be working behind a desk doing a job I hated. I do know that I'm really lucky. I've got a massively successful business that without *TOWIE* I wouldn't have. I've got a lifestyle most people can only dream of, and I'm independent now and can afford to do what I want. It used to be a struggle and I used to panic about money because I didn't have anything to fall back on. Having that worry taken away is a really nice feeling and it's all down to the exposure from the show – I do realise that. I'm not flash with it. I know I'm very fortunate to be earning what I do.

The fame that the show has created for me and other cast members is amazing, and it's been a real platform for so many of us, but it's not always a good thing. Fame doesn't just have a positive impact on your life; there are a lot of negative things that come with being in the public eye too. In a way, I gained a new way of life and financial security, but I lost the one thing that was important to me, the love of my life.

Fame changes some people, but I'm not one of them. I've always been a party diva! No, seriously, my feet are well and truly on the ground, and I am the same person that I was when I started the show. Sometimes it feels like people around me have changed. Obviously, I already mentioned the competition between cast members, but jealousy over the work each of us was getting started to turn nasty. No one was pleased for each other; they were just green with jealousy and it was horrible. Friends are really important to me, but it became so back-stabbing that I didn't know who I could trust in the end. Some people had to have been selling stories. How else would the press know such specific details? That made me nervous. Even now I'm out of the show, things get into the media. I wonder how they did and it makes me question and distrust everyone, which I hate. I tend to wear my heart on my sleeve and have to try really hard not to say stuff to people, just in case.

One time I read that I was supposed to be seeing Ashley Cole, which was ridiculous. I see him out in clubs and that, but I've never been on a date with him. I've never even said hello to him! It's like people think up stuff that's not too offensive, pass it off as a story and then get paid for it. It makes me question who my real friends are and makes me suspicious of them, which is a horrible feeling.

Even with Mark by the end I felt that I couldn't trust information with him. We were still seeing each other when I went for *Dancing on Ice* auditions last May and I knew I couldn't tell him because it would get out. There was a time when I told Mark absolutely everything and I knew that I could trust him, but fame does funny things to people and I didn't want to take the risk that he might tell anyone else, so I said nothing.

I'm a girl's girl, if you know what I mean. Some girls are only friends with blokes and don't have girlfriends. You know the ones I'm talking about? Well, I'm not one of them. I do have girlfriends and couldn't live without them. They are my rocks and I wouldn't swap them for the world. In a way, my friends are my family these days. They are the ones I turn to when I'm in trouble, and my true friends are the ones who stand by me no matter what. Good day or bad day, they are always there, and likewise I will always be there for them. I've probably got a handful of really great friends whom I'd trust with my life. They know me inside out and don't judge me. There's a lot to be said for that, particularly now there's so much sh*t written about me.

Unsurprisingly, I lost a lot of my friends when I was going out with Mark. At first we were so wrapped up in each other that we wanted to spend all our time together, and then because Mark didn't like me going out with my mates, it was difficult for me to have a close set of friends. I do regret letting them go. We'd all meet up at birthday parties and big events, but that was it. That's probably why one of my best friends was Mark's sister, Jessica. His family became a big part of my life and I'd always be having dinner round there. Carol would cook very English meals, like sausage and mash or shepherd's pie or a roast, and we'd sit at the table together and have a laugh. She was my first real friend, I think, and the first girl I went on holiday with. Very sadly, though, we fell out and I'm not sure it can ever be the same again.

Jess was changeable. If she was in a good mood, then we would have such a laugh, but when she was in a bad mood, she wouldn't even speak to me. We always got on, though, until February 2012. We had all been to Faces and I'd spent the evening having my picture taken with fans. I was getting drunker and drunker and put in the wrong PIN on my BlackBerry three times and managed to delete all my BBM numbers. A typical chaotic night out really, but I got the sense that Jess was getting irritated. Nothing was said and we all left together and got a cab.

There was me, Frankie Essex, Sade, a friend of mine and a couple of other girls. I was talking to one of the girls in the back of the cab and she was telling me about a bloke she was seeing. She was upset because his family were putting pressure on their relationship and I said, 'Don't worry – I had shit with Mark's family for ten years.' And that was it. Jess went mad, saying, 'What are you talking about? What are you saying?' I was like, 'Pipe down. You are overreacting.' Then she launched herself at me. I didn't know what the hell was going on, but to stop her and pull her off me, I grabbed her hair. We were rowing and shouting at each other. The cab driver had to pull over, so it kind of spilled out on to the road. As quickly as it had started, though, it stopped and we were both in tears, telling each other that we loved one another and were sorry.

I thought that was it – that that would be the last of it – but it wasn't. We got back to Jess's house and Carol, as usual, was waiting up for her. She used to do the same if Mark and I were out together. She came out on to the driveway in her dressing gown and was like, 'What's going on? What has happened to my daughter?' She thought that Jess and one of the other girls had had a fight; she didn't realise it had been me and Jess at each other. I went back to Sade's house and she started to get picture messages from her mum, Rose, of Jess's bald patch. Apparently, I'd ripped Jess's hair extensions out, which was ridiculous because she already had bald patches from her hair extensions. Rose is best friends with Carol, so she was asking Sade what had gone on. I was so upset I was still shaking from what had happened and didn't understand why pictures of Jess were being taken. I thought we'd made up.

Sade was like, 'If they are taking pictures, then I am gonna take some pictures of your forehead and lip where she bashed you up.' I really couldn't understand the point. What were they trying to say? It had happened, and as far as I was concerned, it was over. End of. We had said sorry to each other and I wanted to forget about it.

The next day Jess and I talked on the phone and agreed that we would never speak about it again. It was embarrassing and I was quite happy to forget about it. Then, a few days later, the story was everywhere. I was crying my eyes out on the phone to the *TOWIE* producers. I thought Jess had given the story to the press, but then she rang me and said to me that she couldn't believe *I* had sold a story. I was like, 'Are you sure? If I had done a story, I would have said it how it happened, rather than what's been written.' She was really upset as she thought I had done this. I wanted to make peace. The last thing I wanted was everyone to know about this. I was sorry that it happened and just wanted to forget it.

I was so pissed off, angry and upset, I can't tell you. I didn't ever really want to have to defend myself on this, but seeing as this story went everywhere and I never had my say, I thought I'd tell my version of events in this book where my words can't be twisted. The only reason I went for her was because she provoked me and I pulled her off. What was I supposed to do? All over again the press made me look like the one in the wrong. Nothing new there, but each time it happens it really f*cks me off and I think, What the hell have I done to you?

Thank God Frankie was there and witnessed the whole thing because she went on the record publicly on *TOWIE* to put the record straight, which I was really grateful for. She said it on camera, but that bit never got shown to the public, so I looked like the bitch. Again, nothing new there. Basically, I couldn't win, so I needed to stop fighting and walk away, and that's what I did – I quit. When I did, I felt free and like the ball and chain tethering me had finally gone. That was in August 2012, after six series. They have left the door open for me to return, which I appreciate and who knows what the future holds? ☺

I still feel upset that Jess and I haven't got back to the friendship we used to have. I used to love Jess – we were great friends and have been since we were kids – but since that night nothing has been the same. We didn't speak for a while; I don't think either of us could bring ourselves to pick up the phone. Now we only really see each other at events. We will be pleasant to one another, but that's about it. I invited her to my birthday party last year and she didn't come, which I suppose says how she feels about me. It is very sad. I saw her last November and she told me that she missed me and that what happened should never have happened but the reality is that it will never be the same again. She will always have a place in my heart but I have a new life now and the Wrights are not a part of it.

We shared some great times that have made us the people we are today, because *TOWIE* wasn't our first taste of fame! When I was growing up, my ambition was to be a performer and singer. In 2006 Jess, our friend Gaby and I auditioned for *The X Factor*. Mark didn't want me to, but for once I did it anyway. It would have been fun if Mark hadn't been on the phone moaning about me doing it every five minutes. Me, Jess and Gaby had formed a band called Funky Chick, but when you say that fast, it sounds like 'f*cking shit', so we changed it to Ruby Blue! I've always loved singing and when I was eighteen, I paid for singing lessons. They cost me £50 an hour, which was a lot. I didn't have any help; I had to pay for them myself. We did really well and got down to the last ten at judges' houses. We so wanted to get through to the live shows and win. Lol. Sharon Osbourne, Louis Walsh and Simon Cowell were the judges, and Sinitta came to boot camp as well. It was great fun and I really enjoyed it, so we were gutted when we didn't get through.

I thought about doing it again but didn't, and then Mark told me that Jess had started up with another band and taken Gaby with her and they had auditioned the following year. I couldn't believe she had done that without telling me. I was really upset, but I didn't say anything. What was the point? I just let it go. They didn't get through anyway. Lol. You see, Jess and I have history and I get really upset when I think we can't ever be friends again. I have tried really hard to build bridges, but I can't make her want to have something to do with me. I wish her all the best, though, and I don't want any trouble for her.

I always think that I have 'celebrity' friends and then I have 'real' friends, and I don't get them confused. There's one thing about this industry that I learned very quickly and that's how fake it is. If you get sucked in and start to believe that the celebrity world is real, then you're an idiot. Too many people do. I could see plenty of *TOWIE* people believing it if they had half the chance. The celebrity world is a bubble that can pop at any time. I go out and I meet journalists and PRs and other celebrities and they treat me like they know me when they don't. It's all so overfamiliar, with them calling me 'love' or 'darling', and I'm thinking,

You don't even know me. It's fine, but it's not reality, and I think a lot of people forget that and it's very easy for this way of life to become normal when it's anything but.

Showbiz parties are great, and five years ago I would never have imagined that I'd be going to them, but the nights I enjoy the most are the ones with my non-showbiz friends. The friends who know me inside out. I don't have a load of mates, but the ones I do have mean a lot to me and I know that I can trust them. Like Sade Ibrahim and Charlotte Lubin. I've known Charlotte for years – since I was about fifteen – and she is one of the few people I have stayed close to. She has seen everything that I have been through with Mark and I know I can totally trust her. She thinks I was mad for putting up with Mark for so long. I like Charlotte a lot because she is such a homely person and is so normal and loving. We always have a laugh, and I think it's quite hard to find nice girls who are fun and not bitchy. A lot of girls can be hard work and demanding, but she accepts me for me and that means a lot.

I always seem to become friends with people I work with, like Donna, my stylist, Lyndsey, my make-up artist, and Lauren, who does a couple of days' work at my salon. They have become great mates. Lauren is the one who stays with me all the time because I hate staying at my flat on my own! Real friends will still be around in five years' time, but how many of these showbiz loveys will be? I wanna keep it real.

I have got celebrity friends, though. I met Katie Price a couple of years ago at Runway, a club in London, when I was out with Lauren Pope for an evening and we got on really well. I know what's written about her, but she surprised me by being quite different to how I thought she would be. We literally sat talking to each other for four hours about everything, even though we had only just met. I talked about Mark and our relationship, and she talked about Pete. I was quite shocked at how open she was considering she had only just met me, but I liked that about her.

Kate has a kind of vulnerability that makes her likeable and it makes me wonder whether her extrovert behaviour at times just covers up a lot of insecurities. I think she genuinely believes that no one likes her and that they love Pete, and I think her behaviour is her way of releasing emotions that she is hiding. I think she just wants and needs to be loved. That's why she always has a boyfriend. She was heartbroken over Pete and doesn't want to be on her own, but now she is, I think she is happier. I think she should have some time being single and enjoying it before she gets into anything else.

That was the first time we had met, but we didn't leave the club until 6.30 a.m. It was a really good night. Kate likes a good time, like me. She loves nothing more than doing karaoke. I do it too, but I prefer to do it at my table rather than on the table! ☺ I went to Liverpool with her once and she was literally standing on top of the table singing! She knows how to have fun.

Some people think I shouldn't hang around with her, but why not? I like her, we get on, and if she sees sh★t written about me, she always gets on to me to see that I'm OK or to ask if I wanna go out. When he denied that he'd been seeing me last year, for example, she asked me if I wanted to go to the *Skyfall* première and said she would get me a ticket. I couldn't go because I had *Dancing on Ice* training early the next day, but it was really nice to be asked. Kate is always talking about her kids, and I think she gets a lot of bad press, but she is just a normal girl with her own insecurities. We have become close and she is a good friend to me.

My friends are particularly important to me because over the years they have become more like my family. As I have grown apart from my mum and dad, my friends have in a funny way taken on that role. Lisa is like a mum and a friend all wrapped up in one to me, and I know that no matter what she will always be there for me. Likewise I will do anything for her. I trust her a hundred per cent.

I see Nicola, my sister, as a friend too. I have always looked up to Nicola and wanted to be like her. She is such a strong woman and would always be the person I'd go to when Mark and I had a row or if I was in trouble. She would comfort me and listen to me, and although she liked Mark, she could never really understand why I was still with him. She would be like, 'Lauren, leave him. Walk away.' She'd make me dinner and give me loads of advice and then the next day we'd be back together. We've had loads of great nights out together. I sometimes worry that the people around me think that I am getting caught up in the celebrity world, but there's no chance of that. I have my own worries. For example, I find it a bit awkward because I feel like some of my friends think that because I'm earning good money, I should pay for things. It always feels strange when we go out to dinner and the bill comes because I never know if I should pick up the tab. It's not like I'm loaded, though. I don't know – it's weird and I find situations like that hard. I want people to like me for me, not because of anything else, and I worry about that all the time. How do I know if people like me for me? How do I know if they just want to use me? People ask me if I can lend them money all the time and I

think, Would you have asked me three years ago? I
don't mind lending money, but I'm not the local cash-
point and I don't like being asked. I prefer to offer it,
and I will always help people if I can. This fame game
makes me well distrusting and I don't like it.

I sometimes have to pinch myself when I think of
what I'm doing and how lucky I am. Not long ago I
was out and Steven Gerrard, the England player, came
up to me and shook my hand and was like, 'I love the
show. I always watch it.' I nearly choked on my vodka.
I couldn't believe it, it was crazy, and I was like, WTF?
It was such a weird feeling. We had some banter and
I couldn't get my head around it. My legs were like
jelly. Lol. And the time I got invited to Jamelia's
birthday party at Movida and swapped numbers with
Pixie Lott after spending the whole evening with her
– that was pretty cool. I forget when I'm with these
people who they are and I just banter with them like
they are my mates. It was the same when I met
Will.i.am. He was just a cool guy and we had a nice
chat.

The most star-struck I've been is when I 'sort of'
met Beyoncé at her perfume launch. I *love* Beyoncé
and really wanted to meet her properly, but unfortu-
nately she had a load of security around her, so I had
to just look at her. ☹

Then there was that time I was late for the *Twilight* première and ended up on the red carpet next to Taylor Lautner and Robert Pattinson! I fancy the pair of them – I definitely wouldn't say no – and I couldn't believe it was happening and that I was actually next to them! It was brilliant. #thegoodtimes

Since I left the show, I haven't seen many of the other guys, but I still BBM Lauren Pope and we chat now and again. She was really good to me when I moved out of Mark's. She had a spare room and had always said to me that if I needed somewhere to go, then I was welcome. That day, when I left his flat for the last time, that's where I went. Lauren was more friendly at the time with Nicola, but the more we hung out together, the friendlier we became and we had a really good laugh. She had not long split from Kirk, so she was single too and said she could do with the company. We used to go out most nights. She still messages me now saying that she has never been out as much as when I lived with her. That was a really fun time and it helped me a lot.

I was hoping Lauren Pope and Katie Price would come down to watch me on *Dancing on Ice*, but sadly they didn't get the chance! I felt like I needed all the support I could get. It's so nerve-racking going out there each week in front of God knows how many people and I was terrified I was going to fall over. I was scared half the time just because of the costumes I had to wear – they are so revealing and that's quite a big challenge for me in itself.

But overall *Dancing on Ice* was such an amazing experience for me and I am gutted that I came out so early on but that's just the way these sorts of shows work. The competition was fierce – everyone was so good. Pamela Anderson left in the first week which was a huge shock to everyone so it just goes to show that it doesn't matter who you are!

I put my all into it and worked so hard which I am incredibly proud of. I was so nervous going out on the ice but my partner Michael was just amazing. He's French and didn't understand a word I said half the time! But we had such good banter and he is an incredible skater.

I want to say a huge thank you to him, my family, my friends and all my fans that supported me and stood by me during the show – I couldn't have done it without them. I feel privileged to have been given such an amazing opportunity and love it that I have learned a new skill – perhaps one day I will be able to show off my moves on the ice to my kids!! Until then though I will definitely keep it up – it's such a good way to stay fit and I really enjoy it.

Jake was an amazing support throughout the show,

he was lovely. I don't know whether Mark watched it, and to be honest, though it might sound harsh, I don't really care. We've both moved on.

Argent and I still speak a fair bit – about twice a week. Although we never talk about Mark, it sometimes feels like he might be fishing for information – like when he called me last summer to see if I was doing *Dancing on Ice*. I often wonder whether he reports back! And when I was seeing Tom, he would ask me loads of questions because Mark wanted to know what was going on and if it was serious between us. Even then he was keeping tabs on me and making sure he knew my business. I've got a lot of time for Arg, and I like it that we still speak, but I know that his number-one loyalty is to Mark and I get that. Hopefully he won't ever have to choose between us.

Arg is still so cut up about Lydia. He really loves her, but there's no going back for them, I don't think. Lydia has moved on. His relationship with Gemma was a bit weird, but they got plenty of coverage and I've got a lot of time for Gemma. She has always been very supportive of me. I think as a bigger girl she sees what people write about me and how much it hurts and she'll often have a go at the people who have said things, which means a lot. ☺

As for Mark, he might have thought I was nothing without him and that I would fizzle out without him, whereas he thinks he's gonna be James Bond or some-thing. I hope deep down he is happy for me. I'm happy for his success, and one day I would like it if we could be friends. Maybe once the infatuation and love have completely gone between us, we can have a much healthier relationship. That would be nice.

The thing is, I genuinely don't care if all this ends tomorrow. I've had a fun time and I'm not gonna be living on the streets. I want kids and I'm gonna want to settle down sooner or later, and that's when all of this will go. I'll become a mum and my children's happi-ness will be my priority. I don't want them thinking that this life is normal, because it's not, and I will do everything to make sure that they know that. I look at Mark's little sister, Natalya, and all she has seen in her life is us lot from *TOWIE* around her and she's like an adult. I want to keep my children as children for as long as possible. Now I'm older I can see what Dad and Julie were trying to do for me. School and educa-tion and being a kid are more important than anything, and so now I think they were probably right all along!

I am still finding it hard to get my head around my own childhood and understand my family. I sometimes think, What the hell is going on? Where have I come from? I don't think I have ever had enough stability in my life, and going forward, I need to deal with that and find my own way, especially now I haven't got Mark any more. I never want my children to feel like that. Because of my childhood, and because my own family was so disjointed, I latched on to Mark's family and became very close to them over the years. That made it hard when we split up – I felt like I'd lost my family and was lonely. I wasn't hugely pally with them by the end, but they had played a big part in my life as I grew up, and of course Jess had been one of my best friends. In some ways it was a relief when Mark and I finally finished, but it was the beginning of a new chapter, and whereas he had his family to turn to, I had to do it alone.

This sounds stupid, but even losing Wrighty was hard. He used to come everywhere with me, and when he was gone, it was like I had lost my baby. It was lonely, but it was the time that I needed to try and straighten out my thoughts and work out what was right and what was wrong and what I really wanted from my future. I suppose I am still mending, and every day has its trials. Like, if I'm ill, I'm used to having Mark around. No matter how bad I felt, he would always make me feel better, but now I have to learn to deal with it on my own. It's small things like that, when I have to learn to take control after being controlled for so long. It's a learning curve and there are good days and bad.

I think the biggest deal for me is learning to be OK on my own, because it does make me panicky. At the beginning of last year I had a really big panic attack and my sister Rihanna had to ring for the ambulance. It was the same sort of feeling that I had had when I heard about the pictures of Mark and Lucy together and when the newspapers claimed I had cheated on Mark. Rihanna and I were watching TV in bed, but she was tapping away on her mobile texting. The noise of her doing it seemed to be getting louder and louder, and as she typed, my heart started to race. My body was shaking, and I began to feel really faint. I was telling Rihanna to help me and I think she was scared because she could see that I was finding it hard to breathe. She called an ambulance; when they arrived, they put a mask on me and I had to try and slow down my breathing. The panic attacks are so frightening when they happen, and there's no real warning. I wasn't in a good place at that time, but I've come a long way since then.

They say everything happens for a reason and I believe that. I didn't have the most settled upbringing but you know what? I'm happy now, and I've done good. Everything that's happened to me has made me stronger. I am the strongest girl you'll come across. I've been in love, cheated on and heartbroken, but it's made me the person I am today. I am a success and am living the dream I always had when I was a little girl.

People might think I'm still secretly pining for Mark and wishing things were different, but honestly I am not. I have moved on. I am dealing with my insecurities and focusing on growing my business and securing my future for the family I crave. I can't wait to meet Mr Right – note there's no 'W' on the front of that surname – and settle down. I'm not jel any more. I really have turned a corner, and there is no going back. #it'snotyourtimeanymoreit'smytime ☺

Picture credits